HOW CHRIST CAME TO CHURCH

An Anthology of the Works of
A. J. Gordon

Edited and mildly modernized by
Ralph I. Tilley

LITS Books
P. O. Box 405
Sellersburg, Indiana 47172

How Christ Came to Church:
An Anthology of the Works of A. J. Gordon
Edited and mildly modernized by Ralph I. Tilley
Copyright © 2013
Ralph I. Tilley

Back cover photo: courtesy of the Gordon College Archives.

ISBN: 978-0-615-91088-8

LITS Books
P.O. Box 405
Sellersburg, Indiana 47172

Ralph I. Tilley is the executive director of Life in the Spirit Ministries and online editor of Life in the Spirit Journal. For further information, contact . . .

www.litsjournal.org
editor@litsjournal.org

This volume is reverently and gratefully dedicated
to the Third Person of the Triune God —
the blessed Holy Spirit.

Contents

Acknowledgements

For this edited anthology, I am grateful to my willing and helpful proofreaders—our daughter, Rochelle Farah, and my wife, Emily. Additionally, I am indebted to Martha Crain, Gordon College archivist/bibliographic librarian, who kindly provided the back cover photo of A. J. Gordon.

Introduction

Adoniram Judson Gordon (1836-1895) is mostly known in contemporary Evangelical circles by two Christian institutions bearing his name: Gordon College and Gordon-Conwell Theological Seminary. Both schools are located in Massachusetts.

However, long before these schools were launched, Dr. Gordon became widely known as the pastor of Clarendon Street Baptist Church, Boston. It was in the early years of his ministry at the church, when Gordon experienced both a remarkable dream and special anointing of the Holy Spirit. These events precipitated a change in his own life and ministry, that would eventually impact thousands around the world.

Gordon traveled in saintly company, and was singularly influenced by godly individuals who contributed to his depth of Christian experience: men such as Frederick B. Meyer (1847-1929), Arthur T. Pierson (1837-1911), and Dwight L. Moody (1837-1899). Dwight Moody once conducted a six-months campaign within three hundred feet of the Clarendon Street Church when Gordon was its pastor. A. T. Pierson was the successor to London's renowned pastor, Charles Spurgeon (1834-1892). As a close and trusted British friend, F. B. Meyer, who authored over forty books, wrote the *Introduction* to Gordon's *The Ministry of the Spirit*. These, and many more highly esteemed men and women, left their mark on this God-thirsty preacher, who in time, would be God's instrument himself in leading untold thousands into a devout relationship with the Lord Jesus Christ.

Every church age presents unique challenges for the man of God; the generation in which Gordon served his Lord was no different.

End time events were being much talked about in Gordon's day. With regard to the doctrine of eschatology, the prevailing teaching was postmillennialism, on the one hand; on the other hand (as in our own day), there were those in some seminaries and pulpits that did not believe in the personal, physical return of Christ to earth for his Church. Gordon became convinced the New Testament taught the imminent return of Christ prior to his millennial reign on earth — thus, he was a convinced premillennialist. And he believed in Christ's personal, physical return as well. He addressed his convictions in full on this subject in his book, *Ecce Venit: Behold He Cometh!* "It is such a momentous event, the coming of the Son of Man in the clouds of heaven — and the contemplation of it so overpowers the imagination, that we can easily understand why, in this age so averse to the supernatural, attempts to explain away its literalness should multiply on every hand."[1]

As a pastor, Gordon faced some cultural issues, which became a sore burden for him: pew rentals, which were filled with the wealthy; and a paid choir, with many members who did not make a profession of faith. He also was troubled in his early years at the Clarendon Street Church over his own spiritual shallowness, and with the same among the majority of his parishioners. God's remedy for all of these concerns — and many more — began with an amazing dream and a powerful anointing of the Holy Spirit. The dream, with its subsequent results, are related in his book, *How Christ Came to Church*, which appears in this volume. And what a moving story it is!

While some of the issues facing churches and church leaders may be different in our day than Gordon's, the fundamental questions remain the same: Is the Lord Jesus Christ, in the person of the Holy Spirit, genuinely and practically *welcome* in my life and church? Will we allow him to be the Administrator, or will we merely treat him as a bystander?

Through the Holy Spirit's personal dealings with him, Gordon became convinced that most ministers and Christians were living beneath their gospel privileges. In reviewing his own walk with Christ and ministerial labors, he came to realize that so much of what he had been engaged in as a minister was done through human effort instead of in the strength and wisdom of the Spirit. He longed for a greater sense of reality in his walk with Christ; he craved a holy heart and a crucified ego; he wanted to be a truly fruitful branch on the Vine.

In the depths of his personal and ministerial desperation—in addition to his God-given dream—the Lord providentially used two men to influence this uneasy, burdened, and conflicted pastor, who were in turn were used to influence his cultured and cold church. The one was a godly member of his own church; the other, a converted shoe salesman and Spirit-filled evangelist from Chicago.

As for the godly church member—a year after his father's death, Ernest Gordon wrote, "Among all the influences, which touched and vivified the early ministry at Clarendon Street, none was stronger than that of Uncle John Vassar, a devoted laborer for souls." A. J. Gordon said of Vassar after his death,

> Far beyond any man whom I ever knew was it true of him that his citizenship was in heaven, and so filled was he with the glory and the power of the heavenly life, that to many he seemed like a foreigner speaking an unknown tongue. I have never been so humbled and quickened by contact with any living man as with him. Hundreds of Christians, while sorrowing that they shall see his face no more for the present, will bless God as long as they live for the inspiration which they have received from his devoted life. . . .
>
> The nights which he spent at my home, were nights of prayer and pleading for my congregation and my ministry. Again and again would I hear him rising in the midnight hours to plead with God for the unsaved, till I had frequently to admonish him that he must not lose his sleep.[2]

Ernest Gordon was later to write of Vassar, "he wrought and prayed and instructed the young minister, meekly teachable before such a master of spiritual things, in those hard-learned and rarely acquired secrets which open the way to the heart of hearts of sinful humanity." Then he makes a telling observation: "The inspiration which this faithful man brought with him accrued principally to the pastor of Clarendon Street."[3]

The Spirit-filled evangelist from Chicago, who was to have such a profound and lasting effect on Gordon and the church, was Dwight L. Moody. "The influence of Mr. Moody's meetings in 1877 affected both pastor and people," writes Ernest Gordon. "Indeed, this year was the turning-point, the climacteric which, after seven years of lethargic religious life, opened a new period of spiritual health. When the revival meetings were finished, Gordon realized that the crest of the hill had been passed, and that the crisis in the struggle for a spiritual as against—a secular church was over."[4]

Because of what Gordon experienced himself, as well as what he witnessed in his pastorate and elsewhere, he preached and wrote much about the ministry of the Holy Spirit. He believed it was the privilege for all of God's people to experience what he termed "the baptism of the Holy Spirit." Gordon taught that this experience was usually—but not necessarily—subsequent to one's initial conversion to Christ. In his writings, he variously calls this experience an enduement, a baptism (with, in, by) of the Spirit, the anointing of the Spirit, and the infilling of the Spirit. While he was not as theologically precise in his use of language regarding this experience as some may wish, nevertheless, no one who was acquainted with A. J. Gordon personally, nor has carefully explored his works, could honestly deny that God had done a mighty work of grace in and through this pastor-evangelist. And history attests to multitudes of Christ's devout followers experiencing a similar encounter with the promised Paraclete.

For myself, I have been greatly blessed in reading after this saintly, full-of-the-Spirit man. While browsing in a Christian used-book store some thirty-five years ago, I spied an original edition of Gordon's *The Ministry of the Spirit*, which I purchased for $1.00! Recently, while re-reading this cherished work and some others by him, I became persuaded that an anthology of his writings should be published. Most of his works are available on the Internet; however, I felt if I could gather some of the "cream" of his works into one hard copy volume, it would be useful to many in the body of Christ.

While there are many theories about the doctrine of sanctification and the ministries of the Holy Spirit, one should not allow a particular doctrinal bias to prevent him and her from being edified by Gordon's beliefs on these matters. Throughout church history, God has periodically raised up a variety of men and women to re-emphasize a *biblical truth* which had long been neglected. Our Lord graciously used A. J. Gordon—and others—in the latter half of the 19th century to remind the Church of her necessary dependence upon the indwelling Spirit for the life and health of the churches. And God continues to use Gordon today, long after his death, through the printed page.

About this edition. In editing and mildly updating the language for this anthology, I have retained Gordon's usage of the *King James Version of the Bible*; to have done otherwise would have diminished the end product. Furthermore, because Gordon rarely provided the sources for his biblical quotations, I have supplied these. I have also inserted birth and death dates for individuals he references (usually, first occurrence only).

One of the blessings in reading after Gordon is to read the many quotations he used from both church history and his contemporaries. However, Gordon rarely provided complete source material in his notes; at times, he provided none. Thus, I have simply preserved what he recorded.

A labor of love. Producing this anthology from A. J. Gordon's works has been a labor of love. In researching and gathering the material for this book, I feel like I have not only come to know the man, but have had my own heart renewed by the Spirit as I pored over his writings. More than once I had to stop and lift my heart toward God in confession, supplication, and praise. Through his works (over a century now since his death), Gordon has unwittingly, but repeatedly, pointed me toward God the Father, who lovingly and mercifully sent his Son into the world; to the Lord Jesus Christ, who loved the church and gave himself for her; and to the blessed Holy Spirit, who is the Father's and the ascended Son's gift to the church. And for this, I hope to thank him in the next world.

Ralph I. Tilley, Editor
Soli Deo Gloria

CHAPTER 1

Biographical Sketch

by A. T. Pierson

His humility and meekness, his frankness and candor, his generosity and gentleness, will always stand out conspicuous in the remembrance of all who knew him best.

— A. T. Pierson (1837-1911)

How simple and brief are the outlines of a human life. And yet only eternity can fill out those outlines, and make visible the unseen mysteries which we call character and influence.

Adoniram Judson Gordon was

born April 19, 1836;
converted to God and baptized in 1852;
lived in New London, Connecticut from 1853 to 1837;
a student at Brown University from 1857 to 1860;
a student at Newton Theological Seminary from 1860 to 1863;
ordained at Jamaica Plain, Mass. (now a neighborhood in
    Boston), June, 1863;
married Maria Hale, October 13, 1863;
moved to Boston, December, 1869;
died February 2, 1895.

This life thus reaches over a period of almost sixty years, and may be roughly divided into three parts, each embracing about twenty years: the first twenty, his growth to manhood; the second twenty, his development as a Bible student and preacher of the Word; and the third period being especially memorable for his maturity as a Spirit-filled teacher and leader.

The character and life of Dr. Gordon are so rich, both in circumstances and implications, so full of lessons in living for generations to come. Gordon will long be remembered as a prince among the preachers and teachers of the modern pulpit. With preachers, as with musicians, there are different and distinct classes, and it is easy to find to which he belongs. Some study to express the Word and mind of God; they are exegetes. Others study their own life and express their own spiritual moods and experiences; they are autobiographers. Others deal in Divine conceptions, but invest them with the interest of their own experiential history; these are witnesses and reach the truest ideal. Dr. Gordon was one of these. No man's preaching was a more faithful exposition of the Word of God. He would have counted it an affront to the Scriptures to use them as a mere convenience to hang his own thoughts on, or caricature them by a misapplication of sacred words. He was both too original in research and too independent in opinion, to become a mere reflector of others' views, like the copyist, or substitute sound for sense, like the dealer in platitudes. He honestly, patiently, and prayerfully studied the Word of God, and then illustrated—we might almost say illuminated—it by his own experience.

No overview of this life must leave out his work as an author. Several of his remarkable contributions to the literature of the age remain, apart from the editorials and more transient articles in the "Watchword" magazine, the religious newspapers, and the "Missionary Review" periodical, he authored *The Ministry of Healing, Coronation Hymnal, Spiritual Autobiography, In Christ, The Two-fold Life, Grace and Glory,* and *Ecce Venit: Behold, He Cometh!* Two have especially to do with the Holy Spirit: *The Ministry of the Spirit,* and *The Holy Spirit in Missions.* But what a wide range and copious treatment, and on what vital themes! It is not too much to say of these books that they constitute religious classics, and ought to form part of every well-furnished library.

In his literary style three things are peculiarly prominent: first, his vigorous and discriminating use of language; secondly, his marvelous power of analysis and antithesis; and thirdly, his simple, natural, forceful illustrations. In these respects his writings will repay anyone for critical and continued study. If the literary productions of any man of this century can in these respects supply a better model for young men who are preparing to preach, we do not know where they are to be found. Dr. Gordon's book, for instance, on *The Ministry of the Spirit*, is so tersely written and so carefully elucidated, that there is scarcely one needless noun or adjective in all the sixty thousand words which compose it; while every page bristles with new and instructive suggestions; and the whole is so reverent and worshipful that it suggests a man consciously treading on holy ground.

Twenty-five years of this serviceable life were spent in the Clarendon Street Baptist Church, Boston. In helping to mold that church into conformity with historic apostolic models was found the crowning work of his life. It implies neither exaggeration of his own merit nor depreciation of the service of any other man, to affirm that it was permitted to him, amid the atmosphere of Unitarianism and liberalism, to build up a believing brotherhood, characterized by as simple worship, pure doctrine, and historic practice as any other in the world.

To those who are familiar with the inner secrets of the life of this church, its central charm is one which is not apparent to the common eye: the administration of the Holy Spirit is there devoutly recognized and practically realized. The beloved pastor sought, and with great success, to impress upon his people the fact that in the body of Christ the Holy Spirit literally though invisibly indwells. He taught hat he is ready, if he finds a willing people, to oversee and administer all that pertains to the affairs of the body of Christ. Furthermore, he believed that, as the Spirit's administration both demands and depends upon cooperation, there must be neither secular men nor secular methods introduced into the practical conduct of Christ's Church, but the Spirit of God must be recognized and realized as the Divine Archbishop finding there his holy office.

It took years to get this practically implemented into the life of the church, but under his persistent teaching and patient pastoral guidance, there came a gradual elimination of worldly elements, and a gradual transformation of the whole church as a working body until it has become a model for other churches, approximating very closely to the apostolic pattern.

Dr. Gordon has written many noble books and pamphlets, but among all the volumes he has produced, this is the most complete and satisfactory. This church is his permanent "living epistle." The golden pen of action, held in the firm hand of an inspired purpose, has been for a quarter of a century writing out its sentences in living deeds, to be known and read of all men. And the greatest problem now awaiting solution is, how far this church is going to prove that the Holy Spirit still administers the body of Christ there. Should these brethren show that they have been inwardly saying, "I am of Dr. Gordon," rather than, "I am of Christ"; and were this church to prove only a sheaf, of which the pastor was the bond, and which when the bond is removed falls apart, it would be a worldwide reproach.

If, on the other hand, it shall not only as an organization survive the pastor's death, but shall preserve jealously the high type of excellence it attained under his ministry; if it shall prove not man-centered but Christ-centered, and shall regard itself as a kind of trustee unto whom the pastor has committed the gospel he preached, the work he began, and the witness he maintained, to be guarded and perpetuated — this survival of the whole work when the workman has gone up higher, will be a testimony to the whole church and the whole world, as mighty and as far-reaching as any witness of its sort in our generation.

It is a growing conviction that the life-work of Dr. Gordon has reached singular completeness, a rounded symmetry and global influence. Nothing seems lacking. In the beauty of Christian character and culture he had so grown into the measure of the stature of the fullness of Christ, that it may be doubted whether the whole communion of believers presented one man more ripe in godliness and usefulness. He was in every sense a great man: great in his mind, in his genius, having not only the administrative but the creative faculty; not only organizing but originating. His versatility was amazing. He would have been great in many spheres. Had he been a judge, with what judicial equity and probity he would have adorned the bench. Had he been a trained musician, what glorious oratorios he might have given to the world. Had he been called to rule an empire, with what mingled ability and urbanity he would have discharged imperial functions.

But if he was not great in the eyes of men, he was great in the eyes of the Lord, and greatest because of his humility. Ordinary progress is from infancy to manhood; but, as Hudson Taylor (1832-1905) says, "Christian progress is in the reverse order: from manhood perpetually backward toward the cradle, becoming a little child again, one of God's little ones, for it is the little ones that get carried in the Father's arms and fondled."

Samuel Coleridge (1772-1834) sagaciously hints that the highest accompaniment of genius in the moral sphere is the carrying forward of the feelings of youth into the period of manhood and old age. Dr. Gordon more than any man I ever knew remained to the last perfectly childlike, while he put away and left behind whatever was childish.

In estimating the character of Dr. Gordon, great stress should be laid on these childlike traits. The man of God was emphatically a child of God. He never lost his simplicity; he rather grew toward it than away from it; there was a perpetual return toward the spirit, attitude, and habit of a babe in Christ. His humility and meekness, his frankness and candor, his generosity and gentleness, will always stand out conspicuous in the remembrance of all who knew him best.

The love that flooded him was, however, a supernatural grace. Seldom do we find such energy of conviction softened by such charity for differing conviction. His creed was steeped in love. He disarmed criticism by magnanimity, and blunted the weapons of controversy by the impregnable armor of an imperturbable equanimity.

While I was with him on one of our missionary tours, he gave voice to certain convictions which met strong opposition. However, one of his most stubborn opponents confessed that he would rather hear Dr. Gordon when he did not agree with him than any other man when he did.

One of the most beautiful features of his work and character was his unconsciousness of the real greatness of his attainment and achievement. When the Spirit of God controls a disciple, growth in grace and power and service becomes so natural and necessary as to be largely unconscious and in a sense involuntary. Great results come without human planning, certainly without human boasting. . . .

This Boston pastor, even at the very last, when his successful pastorate seemed so solitary in its greatness, had no sense of having done any great thing. If the thought of his superb triumph ever was suggested to him by others, he could only answer: "What hath God wrought!" "A man can receive nothing except it be given him from heaven."

It is true, success of such sort as his is always costly. No man ever attains such exceptional godliness, or achieves such exceptional usefulness, without getting a reputation for being eccentric, or as a fanatic, if not a heretic. Aristotle long ago said that there is no great genius without some mixture of madness. Nothing supremely grand or superior was ever wrought except by a soul agitated by some great unrest and caught up with some great purpose. The torrents that are the melting of stainless snows, high up toward heaven, and which rush down the side of the mountain to carry healing waters afar to dry and desert wastes, leave a scarred and torn mountain's breast behind. But, as Keith Falconer (1856-1887) said: "We must not fear to be thought eccentric, for what is eccentricity but being out of the center?" And we must be out of center as to the world if we would be adjusted to that other *Divine Center* of which the world knows nothing.

Such success also costs self-abnegation. The whole raising of our church life depends on the higher standard of our ministry. "Like people, like priest." The ministry is the supreme flower and fruit of church life—as to growth, its sign of consummation; as to fruit, its seed of propagation and reproduction. The ambition after a cultivated ministry flatters pride and carnality. But there is a culture which is fatal to the highest fruitfulness in holy things. The common wild rose has a perfectly developed seed vessel, but the double rose, the triumph of horticulture, has none—the ovaries being by cultivation absorbed into stamen and petal—the beauty of the blossom is at the expense of the fertility of the seed vessel.

There is a type of ministerial scholarship that is destructively critical and proudly intellectual, and hinders soul-saving. Let it not be thought that it cost Dr. Gordon nothing to renounce and resign the proud throne among pulpit orators and biblical scholars which his gifts seemed to offer, and seek simply to be a Spirit-filled man— consenting to be misunderstood, misrepresented, ridiculed, that he might be loyal to the still small voice within his soul!

This beloved brother stands out as a man, a man of a singularly gifted mind, with rare insight into truth and clear methods of thinking and expressing thought. He was a man of large and noble heart, quick in sympathy, stimulated by Divine love, and knowing the "expulsive power of a new affection" for Christ. He was a man of clean, pure tongue, whose speech was seasoned with salt and always with grace, anointed with power. He was a man of blameless life, in whose conduct the Babylonian conspirators would have found as little flaw as in Daniel's.

But he interests us most of all as the man of God, the man of the Book, versed in the Word of God; the "man in Christ" whom we have known since "fourteen years ago," who looked back for his faith to Christ's first advent, and forward for his hope to his second coming. He was a man of the Holy Spirit in whom the Spirit dwelt, and who dwelt in the Spirit, as the air is in us and we in it. And as the man of God, of Christ, of the Spirit—he was in the church, a faithful preacher, loving pastor; and in the world, not of it, yet evermore to it a blessing.

Personally, the writer who pens this loving tribute never thinks of Dr. Gordon without recalling one specially memorable and delightful experience with him in a mission tour among the churches of Old Scotland in 1888. After the World's Conference on Missions in Exeter Hall, London, and while we were en route to the "Eternal City," an invitation came from the Scottish capital. So urgent and earnest was the invitation that we should visit Edinburgh in the interest of missions before the students in the theological schools had scattered for the season. He felt moved to abandon the Continental trip, and we went back from Paris, arriving at Edinburgh in time for a garden party at the grounds of Duncan McLaren, Esq. (1800-1886), on Saturday afternoon, July 14. Then followed in rapid succession colossal meetings in the famous Synod Halls of the Free Church, and United Presbyterian body.

So great was the impression made by Dr. Gordon's knowledge of missions, grasp of the whole subject, and especially his mingled earnestness and unction, that on the 16th of July a crusade was proposed to be undertaken by him and the writer jointly, among the churches of Scotland. The pressure was so great that we yielded to the will of God, and after a week in Edinburgh, with other great meetings in the Synod Halls, we left together, visiting Oban, Inverness, Strathpeffer, Nairn, Forres, Elgin, and Aberdeen, where we spent August 5th. Dr. Gordon then felt called to return to America, and the rest of the tour was without his helpful inspiration. But wherever he went in 1888 he is remembered, and will not be forgotten while this generation lasts. That year the efforts he gave to missions was such that more candidates offered and more money was contributed than in any previous year. Would that such a man could have been spared to make a world tour of missions and carry a like inspiration elsewhere! When we think of such a man, taken from us in his very prime, when we might have counted on twenty years more of service, we can only remember the words of Holy Scripture:

"Be still, and know that I am God" (Psa. 46:10).
"I was dumb with silence" (Psa. 39:2).
"I opened not my mouth because thou didst it" (Psa. 39:9).
"What I do thou knowest not now; but thou shalt know hereafter" (John 13:7).

We have not yet come to the point where we may penetrate the thick darkness where God dwells, and know the secrets of his purpose who does all things well. We can only trust blindly in the promise that all things work together for good to them that love God. "Ye sorrow not as others which have no hope" (1 Thess. 4:13). Sorrow is not forbidden, but a hopeless sorrow is also a faithless sorrow.

We begin the New Testament with Rama, where Rachel's disconsolate grief still echoes, weeping and refusing to be comforted for those who are not. But we are to leave Rama behind as we find him who says: "I am the resurrection and the life" (John 11:25), and move

8

on in his company toward the New Jerusalem.

Even the Psalm of Moses (90:15-16) teaches us a sublime lesson in Divine compensation: "Make us glad according to the days wherein thou hast afflicted us." An inspired prayer is also a prophecy. If we submit cheerfully to him he will give us gladness for every affliction and evil day, and even so great a sorrow as this shall somehow be turned into joy.

Professor Chapell has suggested a most appropriate quotation as the epitaph of this holy man and witness for Christ:

"I think it meet, as long as I am in this tabernacle,
To stir you up by putting you in remembrance;
Knowing that shortly I must put off this my tabernacle,
Even as our Lord Jesus Christ hath shewed me.
Moreover I will endeavor that ye may be able after my decease
To have these things always in remembrance.
For we have not followed cunningly devised fables,
When we made known unto you
The power and coming of our Lord Jesus Christ."
—1 Peter 1:13-16.

Source for Chapter 1: A. J. Gordon, *How Christ Came to Church: The Pastor's Dream, A Spiritual Autobiography* (Originally published in 1895 by American Baptist Publication Society and Fleming H. Revell Company. Retrieved from: http://www.gordon.edu/page.cfm?iPageID= 1805.

CHAPTER 2

How Christ Came to Church:
The Dream

It did not seem at that moment as though I could ever again care or have the smallest curiosity as to what men might say of preaching, worship, or church, if I could only know that he had not been displeased, that he would not withhold his feet from coming again because he had been grieved at what he might have seen or heard.

— A. J. Gordon

Not that I attach any importance to dreams or ever have done so. Of the hundreds which have come in the night season I cannot remember one which has proved to have had any prophetic significance either for good or ill. As a rule moreover, dreams are incongruous rather than serious—a jumble of impossible conditions in which persons and things utterly remote and unconnected are brought together in a single scene. But the one which I now describe was unlike any other within my remembrance, in that it was so orderly in its movement, so consistent in its parts, and so fitly framed together as a whole. I recognize it only as a dream; and yet I confess that the impression of it was so vivid that in spite of myself memory brings it back to me again and again, as though it were an actual occurrence in my personal history.

And yet why should it be told or deliberately committed to print? "I will come to visions and revelations of the Lord" (2 Cor. 12:1), says the apostle. His was undeniably a real, divinely given, and supernat-

11

ural vision. But from the ecstasy of it, wherein he was caught up into paradise and heard unspeakable words, he immediately lets himself down to the common level of discipleship: "Yet of myself I will not glory, but in mine infirmities" (2 Cor. 12:5). God help us to keep to this good confession evermore; and if perchance any unusual lesson is taught even "in thoughts from the visions of the night, when deep sleep falleth on men" (Job 4:13), let us not set ourselves up as the Lord's favorites to whom he has granted special court privileges in the kingdom of heaven. No, the dream is not repeated as though it were a credential of peculiar *saintship*, or as though by it God had favored me with a supernatural revelation; but because it contains a simple and obvious lesson, out of which the entire book which we are now writing has evolved.

It was Saturday night, when wearied from the work of preparing Sunday's sermon, that I fell asleep and the dream came. I was in the pulpit before a full congregation, just ready to begin my sermon, when a stranger entered and passed slowly up the left aisle of the church looking first to the one side and then to the other as though silently asking with his eyes that someone would give him a seat. He had proceeded nearly halfway up the aisle when a gentleman stepped out and offered him a place in his pew, which was quietly accepted. Except for the face and features of the stranger, everything in the scene is distinctly remembered—the number of the pew, the Christian man who offered its hospitality, the exact seat which was occupied. Only the countenance of the visitor could never be recalled. That his face wore a peculiarly serious look, as of one who had known some great sorrow, is clearly impressed on my mind. His bearing too was exceeding humble, his dress poor and plain, and from the beginning to the end of the service he gave the most respectful attention to the preacher. Immediately when I began my sermon, my attention became riveted on this hearer. If I would avert my eyes from him for a moment they would instinctively return to him, so that he held my attention, rather than I held his, till the sermon had ended.

To myself I said constantly, "Who can that stranger be?" And then I mentally resolved to find out by going to him and making his acquaintance as soon as the service was over. But after the benediction had been given, the departing congregation filed into the aisles and before I could reach him the visitor had left the house. The gentleman with whom he had sat remained behind, however; and approaching him with great eagerness, I asked: "Can you tell me who that stranger was who sat in your pew this morning?"

In the most matter-of-fact way, he replied: "Why, do you not know that man? It was Jesus of Nazareth." With a sense of the keenest disappointment I said: "My dear sir, why did you let him go without introducing me to him? I was so desirous to speak with him." And with the same nonchalant air the gentleman replied, "Oh, do not be troubled. He has been here today, and no doubt he will come again."

And now came an indescribable rush of emotion. As when a strong current is suddenly checked, the stream rolls back upon itself and is choked in its own foam, so the intense curiosity which had been going out toward the mysterious hearer now returned upon the preacher: and the Lord himself, whose I am and whom I serve, had been listening to me today.

What was I saying? Was I preaching on some popular theme in order to catch the ear of the public? Well, thank God it was of himself I was speaking. However imperfectly done, it was Christ and him crucified whom I was holding up this morning. But in what spirit did I preach? Was it "Christ crucified preached in a crucified style?" Or did the preacher magnify himself while exalting Christ? So anxious and painful did these questions become that I was about to ask the brother with whom he had sat if the Lord had said anything to him concerning the sermon, but a sense of propriety and self-respect at once checked the suggestion.

Then immediately other questions began with equal vehemence to crowd into the mind. "What did he think of our sanctuary, its gothic arches, its stained windows, its costly and powerful organ? How was he impressed with the music and the order of the worship?" It did not seem at that moment as though I could ever again care or have the smallest curiosity as to what men might say of preaching, worship, or church, if I could only know that he had not been displeased, that he would not withhold his feet from coming again because he had been grieved at what he might have seen or heard.

We speak of "a momentous occasion." This, though in sleep, was recognized as such by the dreamer—a lifetime, almost an eternity of interest crowded into a single solemn moment. One present for an hour who could tell me all I have so longed to know; who could point out to me the imperfections of my service; who could reveal to me my real self, to whom, perhaps, I am most a stranger; who could correct the errors in our worship to which long usage and accepted tradition may have rendered us insensible. While I had been preaching for a half-hour he had been here and listening who could have told me all this and infinitely more—and my eyes had been blind that I knew him not; and now he had gone. "Yet a little while I am with you, and then I go unto him that sent me" (John 7:33).

One thought, however, lingered in my mind with something of comfort and more of awe. "He has been here today, and no doubt he will come again." And mentally repeating these words as one regretfully meditating on a vanished vision, "I awoke, and it was a dream." No, it was not a dream. It was a vision of the deepest reality, a miniature of an actual ministry, verifying the statement often repeated that sometimes we are most awake toward God when we are asleep toward the world.

CHAPTER 3

How Christ Came to Church: Here Today

I had known the Holy Spirit as a heavenly influence to be invoked, but some-how I had not grasped the truth that he is a Person of the Godhead who came down to earth at a definite time and who has been in the church ever since, just as really as Jesus was here during the thirty-three years of his earthly life.

—A. J. Gordon

H ere today, and to come again." In this single sentence the two critical turning points of an extended ministry are marked. It is not what we have but what we know that we have which determines our material or spiritual wealth. A poor farmer owned a piece of hard, rocky land from which, at the price of only the severest toil, he was able to support his family. He died and bequeathed his farm to his eldest son. By an accident the son discovered traces of gold on the land which, being explored, was found to contain mineral wealth of immense value. The father had had precisely the same property which the son now possessed, but while the one lived and died a poor man the other became independently rich. And yet the difference between the two depended entirely upon the fact that the son knew what he had, and the father did not know. "Where two or three are gathered together in my name, there am I in the midst of them," says Christ (Matt. 18:20).

Then the dream was literally true, was it? Yes. If this promise of the Son of God means what it says, Jesus of Nazareth was present not only on that Sunday morning, but on every Sunday morning when his disciples assemble for worship. "Why, then, O preacher, did you not fix your attention on him from the first day you stood up in the congregation as his witness, asking how you might please him before once raising the question how you might please the people, and how in your ministry you might have his help above the help of every other? Was the dream which came to you in the transient visions of the night more real to you than his own promise, 'Lo, I am with you alway,' (Matt. 28:20) which is given in that Word which endures forever?"

Alas, that it was ever so! It is not what we know but what we know that we know which constitutes our spiritual wealth. I must have read and expounded these words of Jesus again and again during my ministry, but somehow for years they had no really practical meaning to me. Then came a blessed and ever-to-be-remembered crisis in my spiritual life when from a deeper insight into Scripture the doctrine of the Holy Spirit began to open to me. Now I apprehended how and in what sense Jesus is present: not in some figurative or even potential sense, but literally and really present in the Holy Spirit, his invisible self. "And I will pray the Father, and he shall give you another Comforter, that he may abide with you for ever" (John 14:16).

The coming of this other Paraclete was conditioned on the departure of Jesus: "if I depart, I will send him unto you" (John 16:7). And this promise was perfectly fulfilled on Pentecost. As truly as Christ went up, the Holy Spirit came down; the one took his place at the Father's right hand in heaven, the other took his seat in the church on earth which is "builded together for a habitation of God in the Spirit" (Eph. 2:22). And yet, lest by this discourse about his going and the Comforter's coming we should be led to think that it is not Christ who is with us, he says, clearly referring to the Spirit: "I will not leave you orphans; I will come to you" (John 14:18). Thus it is made plain that the Lord himself is truly though invisibly here in the midst of every company of disciples gathered in any place in his name.

If Christ came to church and sat in one of the pews, what then? Would not the minister constrain him to preach to the people and allow himself to be a listener? If he were to decline and say: "I am among you as one that heareth," would he not beg him at least to give the congregation some message of his own through the lips of the preacher? If an offering for the spread of the gospel among the heathen were to be asked on that morning, would not the Master be urged to make the plea and to tell the people how he himself "though rich, for our sakes became poor that we through his poverty might be rich" (2 Cor. 8:9). If any strife existed in the flock, would there not be an earnest appeal to him, the Good Shepherd, to guide his own sheep into the right way and to preserve the fold in peace?

Ah, yes. And Christ did come to church and abode there, but we knew it not, and therefore we took all the burden of teaching and collecting and governing on ourselves till we were often wearied with a load too heavy for us to bear. Well do we remember those days when drudgery was pushed to the point of desperation. The hearers must be moved to repentance and confession of Christ; therefore more effort must be devoted to the sermon, more hours to elaborating its points, more pungency put into its sentences, more study bestowed on its delivery. And then came the disappointment that few, if any were converted by all this which had cost a week of solid toil.

And now attention was turned to the prayer meeting as the possible seat of the difficulty — so few attending it and so little readiness to participate in its services. A pulpit scourging must be laid on next Sunday, and the sharpest sting which words can effect put into the lash. Alas, there is no increase in the attendance, and instead of spontaneity in prayer and witnessing there is a silence which seems almost like sullenness! Then the administration goes wrong and opposition is encountered among officials, so that caucusing must be undertaken to get the members to vote as they should. Thus the burdens of anxiety increase while we are trying to lighten them, and should-be helpers become hinderers, till discouragement comes and sleepless nights ensue. These hot boxes on the train of our activities necessitating a stop and a visit to the doctor, with the verdict overwork and the remedy absolute rest.

It was after much of all this of which even the most intimate friends knew nothing, that there came one day a still voice of admonition, saying, "There standeth one among you, whom ye know not" (John 1:26). And perhaps I answered, "Who is he, Lord, that I might know him?" I had known the Holy Spirit as a heavenly influence to be invoked, but somehow I had not grasped the truth that he is a Person of the Godhead who came down to earth at a definite time and who has been in the church ever since, just as really as Jesus was here during the thirty-three years of his earthly life.

Precisely here was the defect. For it may be a question whose loss is the greater, his who thinks that Christ is present with him when he is not, or his who thinks not that Christ is present with him when he is? Recall the story of the missing child Jesus and how it is said that "they supposing him to be in the company went forward a day's journey" (Luke 2:44). Alas, of how many nominal Christians is this true today! They journey on for years, saying prayers, reciting creeds, pronouncing confessions, giving alms, and doing duties, imagining all the time that because of these things Christ is with them. Happy are they if their mistake is not discovered too late for them to retrace their steps and to find, through personal regeneration, the renewed heart which constitutes the absolute essential to companionship with the Son of God.

On the other hand, how many true Christians toil on, bearing burdens and assuming responsibilities far too great for their natural strength, utterly forgetful that the mighty Burden-bearer of the world is with them to do for them and through them that which they have undertaken to accomplish alone! Happy also for these if some weary day the blessed Paraclete, the invisible Christ, shall say to them, "Have I been so long time with you, and yet hast thou not known me" (John 14:9)?

So it happened to the writer. The strong Son of God revealed himself as being evermore in his church, and I knew him, not through a sudden burst of revelation, not through some thrilling experience of instantaneous sanctification, but by a quiet, sure, and steady discovery, increasing more and more. Jesus in the Spirit stood with me in a kind of spiritual epiphany, and just as definitely and irrevocably as I once took Christ crucified as my sin-bearer, I now took the Holy Spirit for my burden-bearer. "Then you received the baptism of the Holy Spirit did you?" someone will ask. Well, we prefer not to use an expression which is not strictly biblical. The great promise, "Ye shall be baptized with the Holy Spirit" (Acts 1:5) was fulfilled on the day of

Pentecost once for all, as it seems to us. Then the Paraclete was given for the entire dispensation, and the whole church present and future was brought into the economy of the Spirit, as it is written: "For in one Spirit were we all baptized into one body" (1 Cor. 12:13 RV).

But for God to give is one thing; for us to receive is quite another. "God so loved that he gave his only begotten Son" (John 3:16), is the Word of our Lord to Nicodemus. But it is written also: "As many as received him to them gave he power to become the sons of God" (John 1:12). In order to experience regeneration and sonship, it is as absolutely essential for us to receive as for God to have given. So on the day of Pentecost the Holy Spirit, as the Comforter, Advocate, Helper, and Teacher and Guide, was given to the church.

The disciples who before had been regenerated by the Spirit, as is commonly held, now received the Holy Spirit to qualify and empower them for service. It was another and higher experience than that which they had hitherto known. It is the difference between the Holy Spirit for renewal and the Holy Spirit for ministry. Even Jesus, begotten by the Holy Spirit and therefore called "the Son of God," did not enter upon his public service till he had been "anointed," or "sealed," with that same Spirit through whom he had been begotten. So of his immediate apostles; so of Paul, who had been converted on the way to Damascus. So of the others mentioned in the Acts, as the Samaritan Christians and the Ephesian disciples (Acts 19:1-8).

And not a few thoughtful students of Scripture maintain that the same order still holds good: that there is such a thing as receiving the Holy Spirit in order to qualify for service. It is not denied that many may have this blessing in immediate connection with their conversion, from which it need not necessarily be separated. Only let it be noted, that as the giving of the Spirit by the Father is plainly spoken of, so distinctly is the receiving of the Spirit on the part of the disciples constantly named in Scripture. When the risen Christ breathed on his disciples and said: "Receive ye the Holy Spirit" (John 20:22), it is an active not a passive reception which is pointed out, as in the invitation: "Whosoever will, let him take the water of life freely" (Rev. 22:17). Here the same word is used as also in the Epistle to the Galatians. "Received ye the Spirit by the works of the law, or by the hearing of faith?" (Gal. 3:2).

God forbid that we should lay claim to any higher attainment than the humblest. We are simply trying to answer, as best we may from Scripture, the question asked above about the baptism of the Holy Spirit. On the whole, and after prolonged study of the Scripture, we cannot resist this conviction: As Christ, the second person of the Godhead, came to earth to make atonement for sin and to give eternal life, and as sinners we must receive him by faith in order to forgiveness and sonship, so the Holy Spirit, the third person of the Godhead, came to the earth to communicate the "power from on high" (Luke 24:49); and we must as believers in like manner receive him by faith in order to be qualified for service. Both gifts have been bestowed, but it is not what we have but what we know that we have by a conscious appropriating faith, which determines our spiritual wealth. Why then should we be satisfied with "the forgiveness of sins, according to the riches of his grace" (Eph. I:7), when the Lord would grant us also "according to the riches of his glory, to be strengthened with might by his Spirit in the inner man" (Eph. 3:16)?

To return to personal experience. I am glad that one of the most conservative, as well as eminent theological professors of our times, has put this matter exactly as I should desire to see it stated. H. C. G. Moule (1841-1920) writes:

> If a reference to personal experience may be permitted, I may indeed here set my seal. Never shall I forget the gain to conscious faith and peace which came to my own soul not long after the first decisive and appropriating view of the crucified Lord as the sinner's sacrifice of peace, from a more intelligent and conscious hold upon the living and most gracious personality of the Holy Spirit through whose mercy the soul had got that view. It was a new development of insight into the love of God. It was a new contact, as it were, with the inner and eternal movements of redeeming love and power, and a new discovery in Divine resources. At such a time of finding gratitude and love and adoration we gain a new, a newly realized reason and motive power and rest.[1]

"A conscious hold upon . . . the personality of the Holy Spirit"; "a newly realized . . . motive power." Such it was; not the sending down of some new power from heaven in answer to long waiting and prayer, but a reception a power already here, but before imperfectly known and appropriated.

Just in front of the study window where I write is a street, above which it is said that a powerful electric current is constantly moving. I cannot see that current: it does not report itself to hearing, or sight, or taste, or smell, and so far as the testimony of the senses is to be taken, I might reasonably discredit its existence. But I see a slender arm, called the trolley, reaching up and touching it; and immediately the car with its heavy load of passengers moves along the track as though seized in the grasp of some mighty giant. The power had been there before, only now the car lays hold of it or is rather laid hold of by it, since it was a touch, not a grip, through which the motion was communicated.

And would it be presumptuous for one to say that he had known something of a similar contact with not merely a Divine force but a Divine person? The change which ensued may be described thus: Instead of praying constantly for the descent of a Divine influence, there was now a surrender, however imperfect, to a Divine and ever-present Being. Instead of a constant effort to make use of the Holy Spirit for doing my work, there arose a clear and abiding conviction that the true secret of service lay in so yielding to the Holy Spirit that he might use me to do his work.

Would that the ideal might be so perfectly realized, that over whatever remains of an earthly ministry — be it shorter or longer — might be written the slightly changed motto of Adolphe Monod (1802-1856): "All through Christ, in the Holy Spirit, for the glory of God. All else is nothing."

CHAPTER 4

How Christ Came to Church: And to Come Again

The godly William Hewitson (1812-1850) declares that the discovery of the scriptural hope of our Lord's second coming wrought in him a change amounting almost to a second conversion. What if another, not presuming to be named in company with this consecrated saint, should nevertheless set his hand and seal to the affirmation that the strongest and most permanent impulse of his ministry came from his apprehension of the blessed hope of our Lord's second coming ?

— A. J. Gordon

The apprehension of the doctrine of Christ's second advent came to me earlier than the realization of the other doctrine, that of his abiding presence in the church in the Holy Spirit. But its discovery constituted a no less distinct crisis in my ministry. "This same Jesus, which is taken up from you into heaven, shall so come in like manner as ye have seen him go into heaven" (Acts 1:11), is the parting promise of Jesus to his disciples, communicated through the two men in white apparel, as a cloud received him out of their sight. When after more than fifty years in glory he breaks the silence and speaks once more in the Revelation, which he gave to his servant John, the post-ascension gospel which he sends opens with, "Behold, he cometh with clouds" (Rev. 1:7), and closes with, "Surely I come quickly" (Rev. 22:20).

Considering the solemn emphasis thus laid upon this doctrine, and considering the great prominence given to it throughout the teaching of our Lord and of his apostles, how was it that for the first five years of my pastoral life it had absolutely no place in my preaching? Undoubtedly the reason lay in the lack of early instruction. Of all the sermons heard from childhood on, I do not remember listening to a single one upon this subject. In the theological course, while this truth had its place indeed, it was taught as in most theological seminaries of this country, according to the post-millennial interpretation. And with the most reverent respect for the teachers holding this view, I must express my mature conviction that, though the doctrine of our Lord's second coming is not ignored in this system, it is placed in such a setting as to render it quite impractical as a theme for preaching and quite inoperative as a motive for Christian living. For if a millennium must intervene before the return of our Lord from heaven, or if the world's conversion must be accomplished before he shall come in his glory, how is it possible for his disciples in this present time to obey his words: "Watch, therefore, for ye know not what hour your Lord shall come " (Matt. 24:42)?

I well remember in my early ministry hearing two humble and consecrated laymen speaking of this hope in the meetings of the church, and urging it upon Christians as the ground of unworldliness and watchfulness of life. Discussion followed with these good brethren, and then a searching of the Scriptures to see if these things were so. They were convinced of this truth. The godly William Hewitson (1812-1850) declares that the discovery of the scriptural hope of our Lord's second coming wrought in him a change amounting almost to a second conversion. What if another, not presuming to be named in company with this consecrated saint, should nevertheless set his hand and seal to the affirmation that the strongest and most permanent impulse of his ministry came from his apprehension of the blessed hope of our Lord's second coming?

But how is it that this doctrine, so plainly and conspicuously written in Scripture, could have remained so long undiscovered? In answering this question we see how little ground we have for glorying over the Jews. They did not recognize Christ in his first advent because they discerned in Scripture only those predictions which announced him as a reigning and conquering Messiah. This conception they wove into a veil of exposition and tradition so thick that when Jesus appeared as the lowly and humble Nazarene they knew him not, but hid as it were their faces from him. And this strong prepossession still obscures their vision so that "even unto this day when Moses is read the veil is upon their heart" (2 Cor. 3:15).

With the larger mass of Gentile Christians the case is just the reverse. They know Christ crucified, and believing that the Cross is to conquer the world and that the preaching of the gospel in the present dispensation is to bring all men to God, they see no need of the personal coming of the Christ as king to subdue all things under his feet and to reign visibly on the earth. This conception in turn has been woven into an elaborate veil of tradition for Gentile believers and "until this day, remains the same veil untaken away" in the reading of the New Testament.

It was not so in the beginning. For three hundred years the church occupied the position of a bride awaiting the return of the bridegroom from heaven. She, meantime, holding herself free from all alliance with this world, was content to fulfill her calling in witnessing for Christ, in suffering with Christ, and thus to accomplish her appointed work of the gathering out of the elect body for the Lord "until he come." A strange and almost grotesque conception to many modern Christians no doubt. But it was while maintaining this attitude that the church moved on most rapidly and irresistibly in her missionary conquests.

Then came the foreshadowing of the great apostasy. The world which had been a foe to the church became her friend and patron. Constantine, the emperor of Rome, became her head, and thus the eyes of Christians began to be withdrawn from him who is "head over all things to his church" (Eph. 1:22). The great and good Augustine (354-430) yielded to the seduction, and was among the first to teach that in the temporal triumph of Christianity the kingdom had already come, though the King with whose return the primitive church had been accustomed to identify, the appearing of the kingdom was still absent. Little by little, as the apostasy deepened, this early hope of Christians became eclipsed till, in the words of Karl Auberlen (1824-1864), "when the church became a harlot she ceased to be a bride who goes forth to meet her Bridegroom," and thus chiliasm disappeared. What moreover would have been deemed an apostasy in the primitive church grew into a tradition and a creed in the post-Nicene church, which creed until this day largely rules the faith of Christians.

Within fifty years, however, there has been a widespread revival of the early teaching on this point, especially among the most eminent evangelists and missionary promoters, until today in a great company of devout Christians, the uplifted gaze is once more visible, and the advent cry "Even so come, Lord Jesus," (Rev. 22:20) is once more heard.

"But tell me," we hear someone saying, "how it is that this doctrine can have such an inspiring and uplifting influence as you claim for it?" We answer, in more ways than can be described in a single chapter.

"The doctrine of the Lord's second coming as it appears in the New Testament," says an eminent Scottish preacher, "is like a lofty mountain which dominates the entire landscape." An admirable illustration! For in such a case, no matter what road you take, no matter what pass you tread, you will find the mountain bursting on your vision at every turn of the way and at every parting of the hills.

What first struck me now, in reading the New Testament, was something like this: Whatever doctrine I was pursuing, whatever precept I was enforcing, I found it beginning and ending in the hope of the Lord's second coming. Is watchfulness amid the allurements of the world enjoined? The exhortation is: "Watch therefore; for ye know not what hour your Lord doth come" (Matt. 24:42). Is patience under trial and injustice counseled? The word is: "Be patient therefore, brethren, unto the coming of the Lord" (James 5:7). Is an ideal church presented concerning whose deportment the apostle "needs not to speak anything"? Its commendation is: "Ye turned to God from idols to serve the living and true God; and to wait for his Son from heaven" (1 Thess. 1:9-10). Is holy living urged? This is the inspiring motive thereto: "That, denying ungodliness and worldly lusts, we should live soberly, righteously, and godly, in this present world; looking for that blessed hope, and the glorious appearing of the great God and our Savior Jesus Christ" (Tit. 2:12-13). All paths of obedience and service lead onward to the mountain. Our command to service bids us "Occupy till I come" (Luke 19:13). In observing the Lord's Supper we " shew the Lord's death till he come" (1 Cor. 11:26). In the injunction to fidelity the Word is that we "keep this commandment without spot, unrebukable, until the appearing of our Lord Jesus Christ" (1 Tim. 6:14). Let any candid reader collate the texts in the New Testament on this subject, and he will see that our statement as to the preeminence of this doctrine is not exaggerated.

To pursue the figure further. As all the roads lead toward the mountain, so conversely the mountain looks out upon all the roads. Take your stand in the doctrine of the Lord's coming and make it your point of observation for viewing Scripture, and your map of re-demption will very soon take shape, and the relation of part to part will become apparent. Just as Christ crucified is the center of soteriol-ogy, so Christ's coming again is the center of eschatology. Place the Savior where the Scriptures place him, on the cross—"who his own self bare our sins in his own body on the tree " (1 Pet. 2:24)—and all the teachings of the ceremonial law become intelligible, and its types and offerings fit together into one harmonious system. God forbid that we should by a grain's weight lesson the emphasis upon Christ crucified. This is the central fact of redemption accomplished. Even so, put Christ's coming into his scriptural place and all the prophecies and Messianic hopes of the Old Testament and the New become in-telligible—the establishment of the kingdom, the restoration of Israel, the renewing of all things. These two centers—Christ crucified and Christ coming—must be rigidly maintained if all the Bible is to be utilized and all its teachings harmonized.

So the writer bears joyful testimony that the discovery of this primitive doctrine of the gospel, the personal, pre-millennial coming of Christ, constituted a new era in his study of the Word of God, and gave an opening—out into vistas of truth before undreamed of. And, moreover, apart from the question of eschatology, it was the means of the deepest and firmest anchoring in all the doctrines of the Evangeli-cal faith. Why should not this be the case? If it is true, as one has said, that "when the smallest doctrine in the body of truth is mutilated it is sure to avenge itself upon the whole system," why should it not be even more certainly the case, that one of the mountain-truths of Scrip-ture being recognized, all neighboring doctrines should be lifted into more distinct prominence around its base? At any event, I confess myself so indebted to this hope in every way, that I cannot measure the loss it would have been to have passed through a ministry of twenty-five years without any knowledge of it.

And as to the relation of this truth to Christian life: Is not an unworldly and single-eyed ministry the supreme need in these days of a materialized civilization and a secularized church? And where shall the most powerful motive to such a ministry be found? No one who reads the New Testament carefully can deny that our Lord has lodged it in the hope of his second coming. We may not see how the doctrine should have that effect; but if he has so ordained, it will certainly be found true in actual experience.

I recall a lecture which I heard some years since from a scholarly preacher in which he aimed to show that Christ's second coming so far from being personal and literal is a spiritual and perpetual fact: that he is coming all the time in civilization, in the diffusion of Christianity, and in the march of human progress. He closed his argument by questioning seriously what practical influence upon Christian life the anticipation of an event so mysterious and so uncertain as to time and circumstance can have.

Being asked to speak, I related a little household incident which had recently occurred. Having gone into the country with my children for a few weeks' vacation, I had planned with them many pleasant diversions and engagements for the holidays, when almost upon my arrival I was summoned back to the city on an important mission. In the disappointment of the children, I said to them: "Children, I am going to the city today. But I shall soon be back again. I may come tomorrow, or the next day, or the day after, or possibly not till the end of the week, but you may expect me any time." It so happened that I was detained until Saturday. But when I returned, I learned that in their eagerness to welcome me back, the children, contrary to their natural instincts, had insisted on having their faces washed every day, and having on their clean clothes and going down to meet me at train time.

"A good story," exclaimed the lecturer, "but it is not an argument." Ah, but is it not ? Human life is often found to be the best expositor of Scripture. He who put most sublime doctrines into parables, drawn from common experience, can often be best understood through some homely household incident. He would have his servants always washed, and clothed in white raiment during his absence. If we believe that he will not return till hundreds of years have elapsed, we may reasonably delay our purification and make no haste to put on our white raiment. But what if his coming is ever imminent? Let this truth be deeply realized and let the parables in which he affirms it become household words to us, and who shall say that it will be without effect? One at least may with all humility testify to its influence in shaping his ministry. Without imparting any somber hue to Christian life; without replacing glory with gloom in the heart which should rejoice evermore, it is enough to say that when the solemn *Maranatha* resounds constantly through the soul, the most powerful impulse is awakened toward our doing with all diligence what he would have us do, and our being with all the heart what he would have us be.

"Then your dream came true, did it?" No, rather it had been true before it was dreamed, and the vision was a kind of résumé of a quar-ter-century ministry. Here now in the Holy Spirit and to come again in person! These were two discoveries which, added to the fundamental truths already realized, brought unspeakable blessing into one Christian experience.

We reiterate emphatically that that night-vision has never been regarded as anything supernatural or extraordinary in itself. Nevertheless there it stands today in the hall of memory, a dream-parable as clean-cut and distinctly outlined as a marble statue, with the legend inwrought in it, "Here today and to come tomorrow," so that in spite of knowledge to the contrary, it comes back again and again as an occurrence of actual history. Call it a dream of mysticism? What if rather it might be named a vision of primitivism?

The most eminent living master of ecclesiastical history, Adolf Harnack (1851-1930), photographing in a single sentence the church of the earliest centuries, says: "Originally the church was the heaven-ly Bride of Christ, the abiding place of the Holy Spirit." Does the reader not see that here is the same twofold conception — Christ inresident in the church by the Spirit; and Christ expected to return in person as the Bridegroom for his bride? This was the church which moved with such rapid and triumphant progress against ancient heathenism. With no power, except the irresistible might of weakness; with no wealth, except the riches of glory inherited through her heavenly citizenship; refusing all compromise with the world, declining all patronage of kings and emperors, she nevertheless went forth conquering and to conquer, till in a few years she had undermined the whole colossal fabric of paganism.

And might not the church of Christ do the same today if she were to return to this primitive idea, and if renouncing her dependence on human resources — wealth and power and social prestige — she were to inscribe upon her banner that ancient motto: "Not by might, nor by power, but by my Spirit, saith the LORD of hosts" (Zech. 4:6)? Such is the train of questioning started by a dream.

CHAPTER 5

How Christ Came to Church:
If I Had Not Come

There must be such a line of Scripture exposition in the sermon that the Spirit shall have free course to ride triumphantly through it in his own chariot — the inspired Word. And there must be in the sermon such windows looking toward "the divine opening" that he may find entrance at every point with suggestions, illuminations, inspirations. Let those who know bear witness whether, when preaching in such a frame, thoughts have not come in, far better than any which we had premeditated — lessons, illustrations, and admonitions suited to the occasion and to the hearer as we could never have imagined them of ourselves.

—A. J. Gordon

To see Christ is to see ourselves by startling contrast. The religious leaders of our Savior's day were sinners before they knew him, but their sin was not manifested. "If I had not come and spoken unto them they had not had sin," said Jesus, "but now they have no cloak for their sin" (John 15:22). The Son of God is *Christus Revelator* before he is *Christus Salvator*. No truer testimony to the Messiahship was ever uttered than that of the Samaritan woman: "Come and see a man that told me all things that ever I did. Is not this the Christ?" (John 4:29).

If Christ came to church it would be a sacred privilege to entertain him, and evermore the aisles which he had walked would be counted holy ground. But are we ready for the revelations which his coming is sure to bring? His glory would certainly manifest our guilt. Ah, yes! And his lowly garb would also rebuke our costly attire, and his deep humility would shame the diamonds on jeweled Christian fingers.

Does the reader remember how, in the dream, I saw him looking first to the one side and then to the other, as he walked up the aisle on that Sunday morning, as though silently begging for a seat? Well, though there had been misgivings and questionings about our system of pew rentals, with the seats so graded that one could read the relative financial standing of the worshipers by noting their position in the broad aisles, the matter had not come home to me as a really serious question till Christ came to church on that morning. Judging by his dress and bearing, it was evident that were he to become a regular attendant, he could not afford the best pew in the house. This was distressing to think of, since I knew from Scripture that he has long since been accorded the highest place in heaven, "angels and authorities and powers being made subject unto him" (1 Pet. 3:22). And there were other things in our worship whose presence caused great searching of our hearts, as soon as the Master of assemblies was recognized as being there.

To translate the dream into plain literal prose: When it became a realized and unquestionable fact that, in the person of the Holy Spirit, Jesus is just as truly in the midst of the church as he once stood in the company of his disciples and "showed them his hands and his feet" (Luke 24:40), then the whole house began to be searched as with a lifted candle. Yes! And he is among us no longer "as one that serveth" (Luke 22:27), but as "a Son over his own house, whose house are we if we hold fast the confidence and the rejoicing of the hope firm unto the end" (Heb. 3:6). We who worship and we who conduct worship are simply his servants to do only what he bids us do, and to speak and act by the guidance of his Spirit.

And judgment began with the pulpit, as that mysterious man in yonder pew looked toward it and listened, though he spoke not a word. The theme had been scriptural and evangelical, as we have already said, but with what spirit was it presented? We have "preached the gospel unto you in the Holy Spirit sent forth from heaven" (1 Pet. 1:12 RV), is almost the only homiletical direction found in Scripture. And yet how deep and searching the words! We are not to use the Holy Spirit in preaching; he is to use us. As the wind pours through the organ pipes, causing their voice to be heard, albeit according to the distinctive tone and pitch of each, so the Spirit speaks through each minister of Christ according to his special gift, that the people may hear the Word of the Lord. Is it not the most subtle temptation which comes to the preacher, that he allow himself to be played upon by some other spirit than the Paraclete? Is not the popular desire for eloquence, for humor, for entertainment, for wit, and originality, moving him before he is aware, to speak for the applause of men rather than for the approval of Christ? Not until the presence in the assembly of the Spirit of the Lord is recognized does this error come painfully home to the conscience. We must not enter into personal experience here, further than to tell the reader how repeatedly we have turned to the following paragraph in the *Journal of John Woolman* (1720-1772), the Quaker, and read and re-read it:

> One day, being under a strong exercise of spirit, I stood up and said some words in meeting, but not keeping close to the Divine opening, I said more than was required of me. Being soon sensible of my error, I was afflicted in mind some weeks, without any light or comfort even to that degree that I could not take satisfaction in anything. I remembered God and was troubled, and in the depth of my distress he had pity on me, and sent the Comforter. . . . Being thus humbled and disciplined under the cross, my understanding became more strengthened to distinguish the pure Spirit which moves inwardly upon the heart, and which taught me to wait in silence, sometimes many weeks together, until I felt that rise which prepares the creature to stand like a trumpet through which the Lord speaks to his flock.

Here is a bit of heart-biography, so archaic and strange to that spirit of unrestrained utterance which characterizes our time, that it almost needs an interpreter to make it intelligible. But if one has ever considered deeply the requirement to speak in the Spirit, its meaning will be very plain. Is it not as true of our spirits as of our bodies that the severest colds which we contract come to us from sitting in a draught? Perhaps a current of popular applause strikes us and before we know it our fervor has become chilled, and then we find ourselves preaching *self* instead of preaching Christ, giving more heed to rhetorical effect than to spiritual impression, till the Lord mercifully humbles us and shows us our sin. Well were it if we could sometimes impose on ourselves the penance of "silence many weeks together" until we should learn to "keep close to the Divine opening."

What was it then that Jesus in the Spirit seemed to demand as he appeared in church that morning? What but the freedom of the place accorded to him who built the house and therefore "hath more honor than the house" (Heb. 3:3). Is it not written that "where the Spirit of the Lord is, there is liberty" (2 Cor. 3:17)? Not liberty for us to do as we wish, but liberty for him to do as he wills. And where is the Spirit now but in the church, his only sanctuary in this dispensation? Let there be no restrictions on his house then, lest — if in his revelation the Spirit shall,

Show us that loving Man
That rules the courts of bliss[2]

coming into our assembly today "poor and in vile raiment" — he shall hear the Word: "Stand thou there or sit here under my footstool"; while to the man with a gold ring and goodly apparel the invitation is given: "Sit thou here in a good place" (James 2:3).

And the Spirit must have equal liberty in the pulpit, so that if he chooses to come into the sermon in the garb of plain and homely speech, he may not be refused a hearing. Indeed, it was just this accusation that came to one unveiled heart as Christ showed himself in yonder pew — the conviction that he might have been *fenced* out of the sermon many times when he had desired to be heard therein, because the discourse had been so elaborately prearranged and so exactly written out that afterthoughts were excluded though they should come direct from him.

Ah, yes, and that was not the deepest revelation. If Christ is present in the pulpit he must think his thoughts through us as well as speak his words by our lips. And what if these thoughts, like their

Master, should be to some hearers like "a root out of a dry ground" (Isa. 53:2), having no beauty that they should desire them? Are you ready, O preacher, to take all the consequences of letting the Lord speak through you as he wills? This may sometimes lead you out of the beaten path of accepted opinion and into ways that seem devious to sacred tradition. And this in turn, though done in humility, may bring upon you the accusation of pride of opinion as though you were saying: "I have more understanding than all my teachers" (Psa. 119:99).

Does the reader know the story of John Tauler (1300-1361), the mystic, and of that anointing and illumination of the Spirit which came to him after he had been for several years an eloquent preacher? He represents some former teacher as chiding him for departing from his instructions. To which he replies: "But if the highest Teacher of all truth comes to a man he must be empty and quit of all else and hear his voice only. Know ye that when this same Master cometh to me he teaches me more in one hour than you and all the doctors from Adam down."

Bold words! Let us reverence our teachers and seek to know how much the Lord has taught us through them. Let the words of commentators, who have prayed and pored over God's holy Word to search out precious ore for us, be honored for all the wealth that they have brought to us, knowing that only "with all saints," can we "comprehend what is the breadth and length and depth and height; and to know of "the love of Christ which passeth knowledge" (Eph. 3:18-19). Nevertheless, it is good sometimes with Tauler "to be empty and quit of all else and hear his voice only."

And that it might be so is perhaps the reason why Christ came to church that day. The world is full of books which demand our study if we would know the mysteries of God. Criticism has set up its "scientific method," declaring that what in the Bible cannot stand the test must be discarded. But while the vendors of learning are crying "Lo here," and "Lo there," the Good Shepherd speaks, saying: "My sheep hear my voice" (John 10:27), and he is still in the fold to care for his own, to lead them into green pastures where the freshest and sweetest truth is found; to make them lie down by still waters in which they may see his own blessed face reflected. Only let not the sheep hear the voice of strangers who know not the truth. Let them hear only Christ.

Christ is not present in the church by his Spirit as critic and censor of the preacher, but as his gracious helper and counselor. Then give him liberty of utterance in your sermon, O man of God! All our acquirements in knowledge of the world, all our mastery of style and expression he will use, if it is surrendered to him. But this is not enough. There must be such a line of Scripture exposition in the sermon that the Spirit shall have free course to ride triumphantly through it in his own chariot—the inspired Word. And there must be in the sermon such windows looking toward "the Divine opening" that he may find entrance at every point with suggestions, illuminations, inspirations.

Let those who know bear witness whether, when preaching in such a frame, thoughts have not come in, far better than any which we had premeditated—lessons, illustrations, and admonitions suited to the occasion and to the hearer as we could never have imagined them of ourselves. "So after many mortifications and failures when going to this warfare at mine own charges," writes one, "I found that on this day I had been at ease and had had liberty in prophesying, and withal had spoken better than I knew, and I said: 'Surely the Lord is in this place and I knew it not.'"

Give me to see thee and to feel
The mutual vision clear;
The things unseen reveal, reveal,
And let me know them near.

CHAPTER 6

How Christ Came to Church: In Thy Light

Jesus is the serious Christ, the faithful and true witness who will never cover up his scars in order to win disciples. Our latter day Christianity would not abolish the cross indeed, but it seeks so to festoon it with flowers, that the offense thereof may be hidden out of sight.

—A. J. Gordon

Within the church of God the quality of actions depends not altogether upon what they are in themselves, but what they are in their relation to Christ. Many things, quite innocent in their proper sphere, become profane when brought into that temple where God, the Holy Spirit, has his dwelling place.

That mysterious stranger who awed me by his presence in church on that morning, is no ascetic. It cannot be forgotten that he once mingled in the festivities of a marriage feast in Cana, and that he drew about him sportive children and took them in his arms and blessed them. "And if Christ is such a one, O preacher, do not make his church a mournful place where we must repress all exhibitions of natural joy and social good cheer, and become as the hypocrites are who disfigure their faces that they may appear unto men to fast." Well spoken counsel, no doubt! Yet Christ is still Christ; and he has never outgrown the print of the nails. So confident of this am I that in dreaming over my dream in waking hours, it always seemed certain to me that, had I come near to him on that memorable Sabbath morning, I should have discerned the marks of his crucifixion in his body. What John the apostle is represented as saying of our Lord still holds true:

Cheerful he was to us:
But let me tell you, sons, he was within
A pensive man, and always had a load
Upon his spirits.

A convivial Christ is not quite the personage that rises up before us in the prophets and in the Gospels. And yet when one observes the pleasant devices for introducing men to him, which abound in the modern church — the music, the feasts, the festivals, and the entertainments — it would seem as though this were a very prevalent conception. No! Jesus is the serious Christ, the faithful and true witness who will never cover up his scars in order to win disciples. Our latter day Christianity would not abolish the cross indeed, but it seeks so to festoon it with flowers, that the offense thereof may be hidden out of sight. If Christ crucified is "unto the Greeks foolishness" (1 Cor. 1:23), why not first present him in some other character if any of this cultured people are among the hearers? But does not the reader remember that when "certain Greeks " came to worship at the feast, saying "we would see Jesus," the first recorded word which the Savior spoke to them was: "Verily, verily, I say unto you, except a corn of wheat fall into the ground and die it abideth alone; but if it die it bringeth forth much fruit (John 12:24), thus presenting the whole deep doctrine of the cross in a single condensed parable?

Never has there been such a laborious attempt to popularize Christ as in the closing years of this nineteenth century. But if the Savior were to come to church and reveal himself to those who have so mistaken his identity, we can well think of his saying: "Behold my hands and my feet that it is I myself; handle me and see" (Luke 24:39). Ah, yes! here are the tokens by which we recognize his real personality. "I perceive that Christ suffered only his wounds to be touched after he had risen from the dead," says Pascal (1623-1662), "as though he would teach us that henceforth we can be united to him only through his sufferings."

38

But it is Christ in the Spirit not Christ in the flesh whom we recognize as dwelling in the church now; and it is the church as a spiritual temple built of living stones, not a material structure fashioned of wood or granite and consecrated to the Lord of which we are now speaking. Yes, and out of this conception came the heart-searching and the house-searching of which we write.

I have told the reader how having in vision recognized Christ as present on that morning, an intense anxiety seized me as to whether everything in the ordering of his house was as he would have it.

There was a choir in yonder gallery, employed at an expense of nearly three thousand dollars, to sing the praises of God in his church. Some of the number were believers; the larger part made no profession of discipleship, and some were confessed disbelievers. But they had fine voices, therefore were they there. No word of criticism can be passed upon them, since they were serving solely by the appointment of the church. But when now the presence of Christ by the Holy Spirit was realized, the minister of the flock began to have pangs of indescribable misgiving about this way of administering the service of song. Had it not been a method long in vogue? Yes. And did it not conform to the general usage of Christian congregations? Yes. Then why have scruples about it? There might have been none but for the presence of that revered Man from heaven. But Christ has come to church: "and who may abide the day of his coming? And who shall stand when he appeareth? For he is like a refiner's fire and like fuller's soap" (Mal. 3:2). And the burning of that fire began from that day, and could never thenceforth be quenched; and the cleansing must now go on to the end.

Does the Scripture deal in poetry or in fact when it says to the church, the body of believers: "Know ye not that ye are the temple of God and that the Spirit of God dwelleth in you" (1 Cor. 3:16)? Into the inner court of that Jewish temple went the high priest alone, once every year, "not without blood" (Heb. 9:7). Not the less rigidly was it required of the common priests who "went into the first tabernacle, accomplishing the service of God" (Heb. 9:6), that they should come first to the brazen altar of sacrifice and then to the laver of cleansing in order to be qualified for their ministry. And these things happened for examples to us. The types are as rigid and unchangeable in their teaching as mathematics. The altar and the laver; the blood and the water—our justification by the cross and our sanctification by the Spirit—these two are absolutely prerequisite and their order is forever fixed. David under the old covenant sought for the true qualification of an acceptable worshiper when he prayed: "Purge me with hyssop and I shall be clean; wash me and I shall be whiter than snow" (Psa. 51:7). It was first the blood and then the water. The exhortation to the worshiper under the new covenant is precisely the same: "Let us draw near . . . having our hearts sprinkled from an evil conscience and having our bodies washed with pure water" (Heb. 10:22). First cleansing by the blood, then sanctification by the Spirit.

The congregation of the regenerate church now constitutes the earthly priesthood under Christ our great High Priest. He could not enter into the holiest in heaven except by his own blood; no more can anyone on earth perform the smallest service in the worship of his house—that "holy temple in the Lord, builded together for a habitation of God through the Spirit" (Eph. 2:22)—who has not been justified by the blood of Christ. This was the deep and abiding conviction which seized one minister of Christ as his eyes were opened by the coming of the Lord to search his sanctuary. And then followed unutterable distress of conscience about this whole grave question. There were those singers standing above the communion table, leading a divinely appointed ministry of song. And yet the question had never been asked whether they had come under the cleansing of the blood of Christ and the renewing of the Holy Spirit; only whether they had fine voices, well trained and harmonious.

The situation brought such burden of soul that sometimes the whole service—the prayer, the praise, the sermon—was gone through with utter indescribable constraint and spiritual repression. When the mind of Christ was sought for in the matter, his voice was heard saying: "God is a Spirit, and they that worship him must worship in Spirit and in truth" (John 4:24). Half the stanzas sung in an ordinary service are such that unconverted persons could not possibly sing them in truth, and none of them could they sing "in the Spirit." Then came the habit of searching for hymns more neutral and more remote from Christian experience, lest I should be the occasion of causing any to speak falsely in God's presence. And more than all, came what

40

may be called a corporate conviction, a taking of blame on behalf of the whole church concerning this matter. For plainly the sin seemed nothing else than simony. The Lord has appointed the Holy Spirit to be the inspirer and director of sacred song in his temple: "Be filled with the Spirit, speaking one to another in psalms and hymns and spiritual songs, singing and making melody with your heart to the Lord " (Eph. 5:18-19 RV). This delight of sacred song is greatly coveted; and they who have wealth say, "We will give you three thousand dollars that you may buy this gift of the Holy Spirit, and may bring in singing men and singing women, the best that can be procured, that the attractions of our sanctuary may not be a whit behind the chiefest in all the city." And it seemed to me that the voice of the Spirit concerning it all would be: "Thy money perish with thee, because thou hast thought that the gift of God may be purchased with money" (Acts 8:20).

Then in thought the vision came back, and yonder silent Christ seemed to speak: "Reach hither thy finger and behold my hands; and reach hither thy hand and thrust it into my side" John 20:27). And while we wondered he reasoned with us saying: "Who think ye that I am, O my brethren? And wherefore came I unto that hour when my soul was exceeding sorrowful, even unto death, was it that you might live delicately and bring in the minstrels to perform before you in my house? Behold they that live delicately are in king's courts; but ye are they whom I have appointed to bear the cross and to fill up that which is behind of the afflictions of Christ for his body's sake, which is the church. The sacrifice of praise, even the fruit of the lips, have I enjoined upon you; but the luxury of sumptuous music, who has required it at your hands? Wherefore do ye spend your money for that which is not bread, when millions are perishing for the bread of life which I have commanded you to bring them; and I still wait to see of the travail of my soul and be satisfied?"

As I heard all this, the whole heart became sick. I thought of churches which were bestowing ten times, and in some instances fifty times as much, for artistic music as they contributed to foreign missions, and I said: "We are believers by the cleansing of the blood and by the indwelling of the Spirit. We have been constituted 'a spiritual house, an holy priesthood to offer up spiritual sacrifices' (1 Pet. 2:5), but instead of using our ministry in humble dependence on the Holy Spirit, we have brought up minstrels from Egypt, that music with its voluptuous swell may take the place of that chastened, self-denying, holy song which no man can learn but they that have been redeemed."

And out of this storm of questioning and misgiving, and all this deep inquisition of conscience, there arose at last one of the calmest, most mature, and most unconquerable convictions of my life. I could never in any circumstance accept a ministry where the worship appointed by God has been so perverted by men. Not in the language of metaphor or of poetry, but in the words of literal truth I hear God saying: "For the temple of God is holy, which temple ye are" (1 Cor. 3:17).

When I can consent to have the communion table moved out into the court of the Gentiles, and call upon the thoughtless and unconverted to receive the sacred elements lying thereon, then I may see the propriety of bringing a choir of unregenerated musical artists into the Holy of Holies of the church, and of committing to their direction the service of song. This conviction rests neither upon prejudice nor preference, but upon the fixed assurance that in the house of God I am servant, not the master, and that I have no alternative but to comply strictly with the Divine arrangements of the church fixed by the Lord himself.

When I had written all this I imagined I heard some reader exclaiming: "Is not this a Pharisee of the Pharisees risen up within the Christian church, and tithing the mint, anise and cummin of religious worship? Is there really any ground for his scruples, or anything practical in his suggestions?" Let this appear in later chapters.

CHAPTER 7

How Christ Came to Church: The Temple of God is Holy

As the Lord Christ, when "there was no room for him in the inn," conde-scended to lie in a manger, so the Lord, the Spirit, when crowded out of pul-pit, and choir, and pew, and seat of authority, may retire into some obscure retreat of his church – heart of a humble saint or home of a hidden disciple – waiting patiently to be invited back to his rightful throne.

— A. J. Gordon

I recall a sermon by President Francis Wayland (1796-1865), preached while I was a student, in which he spoke thus, in brief, about amusements: "You ask me if it is sinful for Christians to play cards. Well, you remember that the Roman soldiers threw dice and cast lots while our Savior was dying on the cross. But you as his disci-ples, had you been present, could not have taken part in that game of chance. And why should you do so now before whose eyes Jesus Christ hath been evidently set forth crucified among you?"

It was a practical and pointed way of setting forth a great princi-ple. The church, which has journeyed on for nearly nineteen hundred years, has never left the crucified Christ behind. I make no reference here to a material sanctuary with the cross and passion – symbols wrought into its ecclesiastical architecture, but to that "holy temple in the Lord "in which we are "builded together for a habitation of God through the Spirit" (Eph. 2:22). It is in this house that we stand during the entire discussion. As we mark on every hand its Divine architecture, we observe that the cross is inwrought with each article of its furniture. In the ordinance through which we enter the temple, we are "baptized into his death" (Rom. 6:3). In the communion which we keep perpetually within its courts, we "do show the Lord's death till he come" (1 Cor. 11:26). In the pulpit where the gospel is proclaimed, "we preach Christ crucified, the power of God and the wisdom of God" (1 Cor. 1:23). In the songs which we sing we offer "the sacrifice of praise to God continually, that is the fruit of our lips" (Heb. 13:15). Thus the crucified One is visible in every service and sacrament of his temple. That solemn stranger in yonder pew did not "cry nor lift up nor cause his voice to be heard" (Isa. 42:2) in his temple; for in each act of worship he had ordained that his Word should be heard, saying: "I am he that liveth and was dead, and behold I am alive for evermore" (Rev. 1:18).

Once standing within this holy temple of the church, a great apostle wept because "the enemies of the cross of Christ" had come in thither (Phil. 3:18). Who were they? Heretics, who had denied the atonement and effaced Christ crucified from their creed? Apostates, who by their fall from grace had "crucified the Son of God afresh" (Heb. 6:6)? No! They were worldlings who had defiled the temple by their unseemly self-indulgences. And has the Lord no occasion to weep as he visits his church today? And do his five bleeding wounds never plead in silent protest against what is done therein ? I speak not of the one congregation into which he came in vision on that memorable Sabbath morning. The encroachments of secularism had advanced quite far enough therein to give occasion for sincere regret at their remembrance. But they were slight in comparison with what we have witnessed elsewhere.

"Know ye not that ye are the temple of God, and that the Spirit of God dwelleth in you? If any man defile the temple of God, him shall God destroy; for the temple of God is holy, which temple ye are" (1 Cor. 3:16-17). We do not judge that the defilement here mentioned is that of personal impurity, in which one sins against his own body by the indulgence of fleshly lusts and passions. Though the words are often applied in this way, there seems to be no good ground for so construing them. It is the corporate body which is spoken of, not the individual body; and to defile the temple of God is to profane that temple by bringing into its precincts idolatrous rights and ceremonies, secular and carnal indulgences, unsanctified amusements and frivolous entertainments to minister to "the lusts of the eyes, the lusts of the flesh, and the pride of life" (1 John 2:16).

Here we shall refer only to what we know as being carried on within the circle of Protestant and Evangelical churches, confessing as we do so, that it is a shame even to speak of the things done by them in public. Nevertheless we must look at the unseemly catalogue: Performers brought from the opera or from the theater on Sunday to regale the ears of the church with some flighty song of artistic musical display; a star violinist dressed in the style of his profession, preparing the way for the sermon by a brilliant and fantastic solo; a curtain drawn across the pulpit platform on a week-night, footlights and scenery brought from the playhouse, and a drama enacted by the young people of the church, ending with a dance by the gayly dressed children; a comic reader filling the pulpit on Monday evening, delivering a caricature sermon amid the convulsive laughter and hand-clapping of the Christians present.

These are but a few acts in the comedy which the god of this world is performing weekly in church assemblies. Taken with the dramatic readings, literary entertainments, amateur theatricals, fairs, frolics, festivals, and lotteries, the story is enough to make the angels of the churches blush, and to give fresh occasion for an apostle's tears while he utters the solemn verdict: "For many walk of whom I have told you often and now tell you even weeping, that they are the enemies of the cross of Christ; whose end is destruction, whose God is their belly, and whose glory is their shame, who mind earthly things" (Phil. 3:18).

It is well known that certain insects conceal their presence by assuming the color of the tree or leaf on which they prey. Church amusements are simply parasites hiding under a religious exterior, while they eat out the life of Christianity. Sacred concerts, church fairs, ecclesiastical entertainments – how well the words sound in the ears of the unwary. But when the Lord appeared walking among the golden candlesticks with countenance like the sun shining in his strength, their real inwardness was instantly revealed. In the midst of the church entertainments, going on for the avowed purpose of winning the world into friendship with Christians; on the walls of the same church, inscribed in letters of gold, were texts of Scripture which the dim religious light had so obscured that few seem to have read them: "If any man love the world, the love of the Father is not in him" (1 John 2:15), and "Know ye not that the friendship of the world is enmity to God" (James 4:4). When the Lord came in, these inscriptions began to gleam out with such a dazzling brightness as the window panes sometimes exhibit under the rays of the setting sun. Then a great horror of being implicated in so-called sacred amusements seized upon one who read these burning texts, so that once on entering a church where such frivolities were going on, he hastened from the house as the aged Apostle John in Ephesus is said to have fled from the bath on discovering that the heretic Cerinthus was present.

If any shall name such scruples phariseeism or religious prudery, then come and let us reason together. Go into a Roman Catholic Church and witness the services which are carried on there, and the question will at once arise, How is it possible that the simple spiritual worship of the primitive church could have degenerated into such a mass of grotesque ceremonies and idolatrous abominations as are here exhibited? The answer is easily found on looking into history. For a while the church was content to occupy the place of holy separation from the world appointed her by the Lord—witnessing for Christ, working for Christ, waiting for Christ.

This austere attitude gave offense to the heathen who had often desired to be friendly with the Christians, and were ready to tolerate their religion if only they would accord some slight token of respect to their own deities—a gesture of reverence or a grain of incense. But all this was rigidly withheld by the disciples of Christ. Not the smallest concession would they make to pagan customs; not a shred would they incorporate into their worship from the heathen ceremonies; and so long as they maintained this spirit, they went forth conquering and to conquer.

Then, upon the enthronement of Constantine (272-337), the sentiment gradually changed, and the notion grew up that in order to convert the heathen it was necessary to conciliate them by conforming somewhat to their customs. The great Augustine also fell under this delusion, and gave his countenance to the engrafting into Christian worship of usages borrowed from the heathen. He said:

> When peace was made (between the emperors of Rome and
> the church) the crowd of Gentiles who were anxious to em-
> brace Christianity were deterred by this, that whereas they
> had been accustomed to pass the holidays in drunkenness
> and feasting before their idols, they could not easily consent
> to forego these most pernicious yet ancient pleasures. It
> seemed good then to our leaders to favor this part of their
> weakness, and for those festivals which they had relin-
> quished, to substitute others in honor of the holy martyrs,
> which they might celebrate with similar luxury, though not
> with the same impiety.[3]

Here is the door opened through which the whole troop of abominations entered — saint worship, idol worship, virgin worship — till in
an incredibly short time the church, which had gone forth to Chris-
tianize the heathen, was found to have become herself completely
paganized. The nineteenth century is presenting almost the exact fac-
simile of the fourth century in this particular. The notion having
grown up that we must entertain men in order to win them to Christ,
every invention for world-pleasing which human ingenuity can de-
vise has been brought forward till the churches in multitudes of instances have been turned into playhouses, with theater boards an-
nouncing the events for the merry season, boldly set up at the doors;
and there is hardly a carnal amusement that can be named, from bil-
liards to dancing, which does not now find a nesting place in Christian sanctuaries. Is it then phariseeism or pessimism to sound the
note of alarm and to predict that at the present fearful rate of progress, the close of this decade may see the Protestant Church as completely assimilated to nineteenth century secularism as the Roman
Catholic Church was assimilated to fourth century paganism?

And this is not all: the temple has been defiled. "For what agree-
ment hath the temple of God with idols; for ye are the temple of God:
as God hath said, 'I will dwell in them and walk in them, and I will be
their God and they shall be my people'" (2 Cor. 6:16). Anything
thrust into God's place is an idol. When, in 2 Thessalonians 2:3-4, the

culmination of the predicted apostasy is described, it is said of "the man of sin," that "He as God sitteth in the temple of God, showing himself that he is God." Here, I believe, we have a picture of the pope, thrusting himself into the seat of the Holy Spirit, assuming the title of "Vicar of Christ," which belongs only to that "other Paraclete" whom Jesus promised to send down to fill his place during his absence.

This sin of *unseating* the Holy Spirit in his own temple is so blasphemous that its author has no forgiveness, but is doomed to be destroyed "by the brightness of Christ's coming" (2 Thess. 2:8). And is there no danger that Protestantism may fall under the same guilt? What if the Holy Spirit is ejected from the choir, and his office as inspirer of sacred song committed to a quartette of unconverted musical artists? What if he be unseated from the pulpit and the intellectual discourse substituted for that preaching of the gospel "with the Holy Spirit sent down from heaven" (1 Pet. 1:12), which God has appointed? What if he be set aside from the administration of the church, so that, for example, the settling of a pastor shall be made to turn on the votes of unconverted men called "the society," when the Lord has spoken about "the flock of God over which the Holy Spirit hath made you overseers" (Acts 20:28)?

Is there no peril that by this constant unseating of the Spirit he may be finally driven from his sanctuary, repeating as he retires the solemn lament of the Savior: "Behold your house is left unto you desolate" (Matt. 23:38)? Wonderful indeed is the patience of the Comforter! As the Lord Christ, when "there was no room for him in the inn," condescended to lie in a manger, so the Lord, the Spirit, when crowded out of pulpit, and choir, and pew, and seat of authority, may retire into some obscure retreat of his church — heart of a humble saint or home of a hidden disciple — waiting patiently to be invited back to his rightful throne.

That he may, and sometimes does, finally withdraw from his temple, there can be no question. Do we not know of churches once fervently evangelical, which are now lying under the doom of desertion by the Spirit? The writer thinks, with all charity, that he has seen such — churches upon which the Lord's sentence has gone forth, "Thou hast a name that thou livest and art dead" (Rev. 3:1). The body may still remain indeed, the Creeds and Confessions may continue intact, and the forms of worship may even be multiplied and vastly "enriched" as the years go on, but these outward forms are only memorials of a departed glory, like the death mask which preserves the mold of features which have long since crumbled into dust.

If any reader thinks that what we are saying is simply "exposition," we have to add that it is this and more; it is experience, and every word is confirmed in the mouth of heart-witnesses and conscience-witnesses and church-witnesses. When an evangelist goes to a congregation to hold special services, and finds after a day or two that the whole membership is in a state of suspended animation, let him take a candle, as the Hebrews did on the eve of Passover, and let him diligently search the house for leaven. Let him go into the choir gallery and learn whether a quartette of unsanctified musicians is seated there; let him then go into the vestry and inquire whether the winter's program of church amusements is still proceeding.

He may go further, but the writer bears solemn witness that even these two obstructions have been found sufficient to bar the way to all success in revival effort. It is written and cannot, without infinite peril, be forgotten, that the church is "an holy temple in the Lord"; that it is "builded together for an habitation of God in the Spirit"; that "the Lord is that Spirit" (Eph. 2:21-22), governing and administering therein with sovereign authority, and that only "where the Spirit of the Lord is there is liberty" (2 Cor. 3:17).

Except he has sanctified instruments in every part of the house, he cannot move through the assemblies in victorious freedom of service. Yet, so inveterate is the tendency to turn away from the Spirit and to listen to other voices, that "He that hath the seven Spirits of God" (Rev. 3:1), warns his church from heaven in a seven-fold admonition repeated at the end of each succeeding chapter in her seven-fold apocalyptic history: "He that hath an ear let him hear what the Spirit saith unto the churches" (Rev. 2:7, 11, 17, 29; 3:6, 13, 22).

CHAPTER 8

How Christ Came to Church: Cleansing the Temple

The prayer meeting soon passed beyond the necessity of being sustained and became the most helpful nourisher and sustainer of the church. The place is always filled, and instead of urging the people to come, or inviting them to participate, the attendance is joyfully voluntary, and the praying and testifying always so spontaneous and hearty that one can scarce remember when it has been found needful to urge Christians to exercise these privileges.
— A. J. Gordon

W hy not withdraw from the church which has become thus secularized and desecrated? To which we reply emphatically: Until the Holy Spirit withdraws we are not called upon to do so. And he is infinitely patient, abiding still in his house so long as there are two or three who gather in Christ's name to constitute a *templum in templo*, a sanctuary within a sanctuary, where he may find a home.

What the lungs are to the air the church is to the Holy Spirit; and each individual believer is like a cell in those lungs. If every cell is open and unobstructed the whole body is full of light; but if through a sudden cold, congestion sets in, so that the larger number of these cells are closed, then the entire burden of breathing is thrown upon the few which remain unobstructed. With redoubled activity these now inhale and exhale the air, till convalescence shall return.

So we strongly believe that a few Spirit-filled disciples are sufficient to save a church; that does bring back recovery and health to the entire body. I saw no whip of small cords in the hands of that pilgrim-Christ who turned aside for a moment to visit our sanctuary on that ever-remembered Lord's Day morning. The time has not yet come for judging and punishing those who defile the temple of God. On the contrary, it seems as though I heard that gracious stranger say: "Behold, I stand at the door, and knock: if any man hear my voice, and open the door, I will come in to him, and will sup with him, and he with me" (Rev. 3:20). The throne room of the church where he has ordained to rule his flock, the choir room where he would preside in the Holy Spirit as the inspirer of praise, the pews into which he would have freedom of entrance, even when coming in the lowliest garb — these he did not storm with violent anathemas, but gently solicited to open unto him. Woe to those who judge before the time, who depart from their brethren, and slam that door behind them before which Jesus is gently knocking; who spew the church out of their mouths while he, though rebuking it, still loves it and owns it and invites it to sup with him.

"For the law of the Spirit of life in Christ Jesus hath made me free from the law of sin and death" (Rom. 8:2), writes the apostle. This is the method of the Lord's present work — death overcome by life. "I cannot sweep the darkness out but I can shine it out," said John Newton (1725-1807). We cannot scourge dead works out of the church, but we can live them out. If we accuse the church with having the pneumonia, let us who are individual air cells in that church, breathe deeply and wait patiently and pray believingly, and one after another the obstructed cells will open to the Spirit till convalescence is reestablished in every part.

With the deepest humility the writer here sets his seal of verifying experience. When the truth of the *in-residence* of the Spirit and of his *presiding* in the church of God became a living conviction, then began a constant magnifying of him in his offices. Several sermons were preached yearly setting forth the privileges and duties of Christians under his administration. Special seasons of daily prayer were set apart, extending sometimes over several weeks, during which continual intercession was made for the power of the Holy Spirit. It was not so much prayer for particular blessings as an effort to get into fellowship with the Spirit and to be brought into unreserved surrender to his life and acting. The circle of those thus praying was thus constantly enlarged. Then gradually, the result appeared in the whole church; the incoming tide began to fill the bays and inlets, and as it did so the driftwood was dislodged and floated away. Ecclesiastical amusements dropped off, not so much by the denunciation from the pulpit, as by the displacement of the deepening life. The service of song was quietly surrendered back to the congregation and, instead of the select choir, the church — who constitute the true Levites as well as the appointed priesthood of the New Dispensation — took up the sacrifice of praise anew and filled the house with their song. As noiselessly and irresistibly as the ascending sap displaces the dead leaves which have clung all winter long to the trees, so quietly did the incoming Spirit seem to crowd off the traditional usages which had hindered our liberty.

Later came the abolition of pew rentals and the disuse of church sales for raising money for missions and other charities. Meantime the pulpit acquired a liberty before unknown; the outward hampering being removed, the inward help became more and more apparent, and the preacher felt himself constantly drawn out instead of being perpetually repressed as in previous years.

The prayer meeting soon passed beyond the necessity of being *sustained* and became the most helpful nourisher and sustainer of the church. The place is always filled, and instead of urging the people to come, or inviting them to participate, the attendance is joyfully voluntary, and the praying and testifying always so spontaneous and hearty that one can scarce remember when it has been found needful to urge Christians to exercise these privileges.

It is by no means affirmed that the old leaven has been completely purged out, so that nothing of the secular and unspiritual remains in the temple of the Spirit where we worship. No! If that Divine Visitant were to appear once more in yonder pew, and with those eyes which are like a flame of fire were to search our sanctuary, it pains me to think what he might discover, which has hitherto escaped our search. We are only speaking now of a comparative cleansing, deeply sensible of much, both known and unknown, which yet remains to be accomplished.

But of the result thus far may we speak without glorying. Most apt is Dr. Andrew Bonar's (1810-1892) story of the auctioneer, who was commending in glowing words a picture by one of the old masters, himself meanwhile standing behind the painting which he was selling, and allowing it to hide him from view. All that we are trying to do in this chapter is to magnify the work of an old Master, the Galilean Carpenter, who only asked liberty to work among us that he might build "his own house; whose house are we, if we hold fast the confidence and the rejoicing of the hope firm unto the end" (Heb. 3:6). Let his work appear unto his servants, and let "the workers together with him" be hidden from view.

I observed neither saw, hammer, nor plane in his hand when he came into yonder pew on that morning; and though from that day he began to reconstruct the temple, "there was neither hammer, nor axe, nor any tool of iron, heard in the house while it was building" (1 Kgs. 6:7). All went on noiselessly, so that now we wonder at the progress of the work. One freshly anointed was moved to undertake a mission to the Jews, among whom up to this time no systematic effort had been made; the result—hundreds of Hebrews reached by the gospel, not a few converts won to Christ, and a Jewish missionary raised up for his people.

Another brother was drawn out on behalf of the Chinese; the result—a Chinese mission school of two hundred; twenty-five now members of the church, and one of their number, a veritable apostle, now returned to his native land, to make known the gospel to his countrymen. A newly renewed disciple was drawn to the work of outdoor preaching; the result—a band of young men and women raised up who have gone to wharves, car stables, and public squares, with increasing devotion to this service, which has now gone on weekly for more than five years. Others were moved to enter into rescue work among ruined women; the result—a home opened and now a far-reaching effort extending out and bringing Christians of all names into cooperation.

An industrial home was instituted for intemperate and unemployed men; the result—a shelter in which thousands have found refuge, and converts have been won to Christ by hundreds. A training school for evangelists was opened [now Gordon-Conwell Seminary], designed to equip men and women of humble attainments for

Christian work at home and abroad; the result—a score of foreign missionaries sent out since the work began, four years ago. And many more have been sent to destitute fields at home, while a hundred and fifty are now under instruction.

Meantime evangelistic efforts have reached out on every side, some tens of our brothers and sisters being entirely occupied in this work and as many more working in the foreign field. By spontaneous freewill giving the offerings to foreign missions have steadily increased, rising to ten thousand, to twelve thousand, and one year to twenty thousand dollars, as the annual contribution to this work.

And this increase in giving was not the result of begging or pestering. Much prayer was made and the strongest evangelical motive urged in behalf of it. Meantime there has been a freshness and heartiness in our worship before unknown. The Spirit has had liberty to break forth in song in unexpected ways now and then, as when a joyous young disciple going down to be baptized sang the strains of "My Jesus, I love Thee, I Know Thou Art Mine," as her feet touched the water, all the congregation uniting with overpowering effect. What could that little paid quartette have done like this?

So, likewise, there has been an open window into the sermon through which the Holy Spirit has come in with unexpected suggestions, suited for the occasion. In a word, the law of liberty seems to have largely supplemented machinery and organization. And yet, be it noted, that even this record would not be committed to print save for one reason—that it is recognized to be not a *work* but his *workmanship*. Not one of these enterprises was planned beforehand, so that they could be credited to some superior organizer. They *grew up, he knows not how*, who now tells the story. They are described after much hesitation, and with prolonged weighing of each statement, with the hope that they may bring home the suggestion to some who have not entertained it, that the Holy Spirit, the present Christ, has been given to be the administrator of the church; and that in these days of endless organizations and multiplied secular machinery, he will surprise us by showing what he will do if we will give him unhindered liberty of action in his own House.

Source for Chapters 2-8: A. J. Gordon, *How Christ Came to Church: The Pastor's Dream, A Spiritual Autobiography* (Originally published in 1895 by American Baptist Publication Society and Fleming H. Revell Company. Retrieved from: http://www.gordon.edu/page.cfm?iPageID= 1805.

Note: The original volume of *How Christ Came to Church* contained a concluding part, authored by A. T. Pierson: *The Life Story: The Dream as Interpreting the Man.*

CHAPTER 9

The Advent of the Spirit

Therefore the Holy Ghost on this day — Pentecost — descended into the temple of his apostles, which he had prepared for himself, as a shower of sanctification, appearing no more as a transient visitor, but as a perpetual Comforter and as an eternal inhabitant. He came therefore on this day to his disciples, no longer by the grace of visitation and operation, but by the very presence of his majesty.

— Augustine (354-430)

"F or the Holy Spirit was not yet," is the more than surprising saying of Jesus when speaking of "the Spirit which they that believe on him should receive" (John 7:39). Had not the Spirit been seen descending upon Jesus like a dove at his baptism, and remaining on him? Had he not been the Divine agent in creation, and in the illumination and inspiration of the patriarchs and prophets and seers of the old dispensation? How then could Jesus say that he "was not yet given," as the words read in our Authorized Version?

The answer to this question furnishes our best point of departure for an intelligent study of the doctrine of the Spirit. Augustine calls the day of Pentecost the *dies natalis* of the Holy Spirit, for the same reason that the day when Mary "brought forth her first-born son" (Luke 2:7) we name the birthday of Jesus Christ. Yet Jesus had existed before he lay in the cradle at Bethlehem; he was "in the beginning with God" (John 1:2); he was the agent in creation. By him all things were. But on the day of his birth he became incarnate, that in the flesh he might fulfill his great ministry as the Apostle and High

Priest of our confession, manifesting God to men, and making himself an offering for the sins of the world. Not until after his birth in Bethlehem was Jesus in the world in his official capacity, in his Divine ministry as mediator between man and God. And so not till after the day of Pentecost was the Holy Spirit in the world in his official sphere, as mediator between men and Christ. In the following senses then is Augustine's saying true, which calls Pentecost "the birthday of the Spirit."

1. The Holy Spirit, from that time on, took up his residence on earth. The Christian Church throughout all this dispensation is the home of the Spirit as truly as heaven, during this same period, is the home of Jesus Christ. This is according to that sublime word of Jesus, called by one "the highest promise which can be made to man": "If a man love me he will keep my words: and my Father will love him, and we will come unto him, *and make our abode with him*" (John 14:23). This promise was fulfilled at Pentecost, and the first two Persons of the Godhead now hold residence in the church through the Third.

The Holy Spirit during the present time is in office on earth; and all spiritual presence and divine communion of the Trinity with men are through him. In other words, while the Father and the Son are visibly and personally in heaven, they are invisibly here in the body of the faithful by the indwelling of the Comforter. So that though we affirm that on the day of Pentecost the Holy Spirit came to dwell upon earth for this entire dispensation, we do not imply that he thereby ceased to be in heaven. Not with God, as with finite man, does arrival in one place necessitate withdrawal from another.

Jesus uttered a saying concerning himself so mysterious and seemingly contradictory that many attempts have been made to explain away its literal and obvious meaning: "And no man hath ascended up to heaven but he that came down from heaven, even the Son of man who is in heaven" (John 3:13). Christ was on earth, and yet in glory; here and there, at the same time—just as a thought, which we embody in speech and send forth from the mind, yet remains in the mind as really and distinctly as before it was expressed. Why should this saying concerning our Divine Lord seem incredible? And as with the Son, so with the Spirit. The Holy Spirit is here, abiding perpetually in the church; and he is likewise there, in communion with the Father and the Son from whom he proceeds, and from whom, as coequal partner in the Godhead, he can never be separated any more than the sunbeam can be dissociated from the sun in which it has its source.

2. Again, the Holy Spirit, in a mystical but very real sense, became embodied in the church on the day of Pentecost. Not that we would by any means put this embodiment on the same plane with the incarnation of the Second Person of the Trinity. When "the Word was made flesh and dwelt among us (John 1:14), it was God entering into union with sinless humanity; here it is the Holy Spirit uniting himself with the church in its imperfect and militant condition. Nevertheless, it is according to literal Scripture that the body of the faithful is indwelt by the Divine Spirit. In this fact we have the distinguishing peculiarity of the present dispensation. "For he dwelleth with you, and shall be in you" (John 14:17), said Jesus, speaking anticipatively of the coming of the Comforter.

And so truly was this prediction fulfilled that ever after the day of Pentecost the Holy Spirit is spoken of as being in the church. "If so be that the Spirit of God dwell in you" (Rom. 8:9) is the inspired assumption on which the deep teaching in Romans 8 proceeds. All the recognition and deference which the disciples paid to their Lord they now pay to the Holy Spirit, his true vicar, his invisible self, present in the body of believers. How artlessly and naturally this comes out in the conclusions of the first council at Jerusalem: "It seemed good to the Holy Spirit and to us" (Acts 15:28) runs the record; as though it had been said: "Peter and James and Barnabas and Saul and the rest were present, and also just as truly was the Holy Spirit."

And when the first capital sin was committed in the church, in the conspiracy and falsehood of Ananias and Sapphira, Peter's question is: "Why hath Satan filled thine heart to lie to the Holy Spirit?" "How is it that ye have agreed together to tempt the Holy Spirit?" (Acts 5:3, 9). Not only is the personal presence of the Spirit in the body of believers thus distinctly recognized, but he is there in authority and supremacy, as the center of the assembly. "Incarnated in the church!" do we say? We get this conception by comparing together

59

the inspired characterizations of Christ and of the church. "This temple" (John 2:19) was the name which he gave to his own Divine person, greatly to the scandal and indignation of the Jews; and the evangelist explains to us that "he spoke of the temple of his body" (John 2:21) A metaphor, a type, do we say?

No! He said so because it was so. "The Word was made flesh and tabernacled among us, and we beheld his glory" (John 1:14). This is temple imagery. "Tabernacled" is the word used in Scripture for the dwelling of God with men; and the temple is God's dwelling place. The "glory" harmonizes with the same idea. As the *Shechinah* cloud rested above the mercy seat, the symbol and sign of God's presence, so from the Holy of Holies of our blessed Lord's heart did the glory of God shine forth, "the glory as of the only begotten of the Father, full of grace and truth" (John 1:14), certifying him to be the veritable temple of the Most High.

After his ascension and the sending down of the Spirit, the church takes the name her Lord had borne before — she is the temple of God, and the only temple which he has on earth during the present dispensation. "Know ye not that ye are the temple of God, and that the Spirit of God dwelleth in you?" (1 Cor. 3:16), asks the apostle. This he speaks to the church in its corporate capacity. "A holy temple in the Lord, in whom ye also are builded together for a habitation of God through the Spirit" (Eph. 2:22), is the sublime description in the Epistle to the Ephesians.

It is enough that we now emphasize the fact that the same language is here applied to the church which Christ applies to himself. As with the Head, so with the mystical body; each is indwelt by the Holy Spirit, and thus is God in some sense incarnated in both; and for the same reason. Christ was "the image of the invisible God" (Col. 1:15); and when he stood before men in the flesh he could say to them, "He that hath seen me hath seen the Father" (John 14:9).

Not otherwise than through the incarnation, so far as we know, could the unknown God become known, and the unseen God become seen. So, after Christ had returned to the Father, and the world saw him no more, he sent the Paraclete to be incarnated in his mystical body, the church. As the Father revealed himself through the Son, so the Son by the Holy Spirit now reveals himself through the church.

As Christ was the image of the invisible God, so the church is appointed to be the image of the invisible Christ; and his members, when they are glorified with him, shall be the express image of his person.

This then is the mystery and the glory of this dispensation; not less true because mysterious; not less practical because glorious. In an admirable work on the Spirit, the distinction between the former and the present relation of the Spirit is thus stated:

> In the old dispensation the Holy Spirit wrought *upon* believers, but did not in his person dwell *in* believers and abide permanently in them. He *appeared* unto men; he did not incarnate himself *in* man. His action was intermittent; he went and came like the dove which Noah sent forth from the ark, and which went to and fro, finding no rest; while in the new dispensation he dwells, he abides in the heart as the dove, his emblem, which John saw descending and alighting on the head of Jesus. Pledged to the soul, the Spirit went oft to see his betrothed, but was not yet one with her; the marriage was not consummated until Pentecost, after the glorification of Jesus Christ.[1]

3. A still more obvious reason why before the day of Pentecost it could be said that "the Holy Spirit was not yet," is contained in the words, "because that Jesus was not yet glorified" (John 7:39). In the order of the unfolding ages we see each of the persons of the Godhead in turn exercising an earthly ministry and dealing with man in the work of redemption. Under the law, God the Father comes down to earth and speaks to men from the cloud of Sinai and from the glory above the mercy seat. Under grace, God the Son is in the world, teaching, suffering, dying, and rising again. Under the dispensation of election and out-gathering now going on, the Holy Spirit is here carrying on the work of renewing and sanctifying the church, which is the body of Christ.

There is a necessary succession in these Divine ministries, both in time and in character. In the days of Moses it might have been said: "Christ is not yet," because the economy of God-Jehovah was not completed. The law must first be given, with its sacrifices and types and ceremonies and shadows; man must be put on trial under the law, till the appointed time of his schooling should be completed. *Then* must Christ come to fulfill all types and terminate all sacrifices in himself—to do for us "what the law could not do in that it was weak through the flesh" (Rom. 8:3), and to become "the end of the law for righteousness to everyone that believeth" (Rom. 10:4). When in turn Christ had completed his redemption-work by dying on the cross for our sins, and rising again from the dead for our justification, and had taken his place at God's right hand for perpetual intercession, *then* the Holy Spirit came down to communicate and reveal to the church the finished work of Christ. In a word, as God the Son fulfills to men the work of God the Father, so God the Holy Spirit reveals to human hearts the work of God the Son.

There is a holy deference, if we may so say, between the Persons of the Trinity in regard to their respective ministries. When Christ was in office on earth, the Father commends us to him, speaking from heaven and saying: "This is my beloved Son: hear ye him" (Mark 9:7). When the Holy Spirit had entered upon his earthly office, Christ commends us to him, speaking again from heaven with sevenfold reiteration, saying: "He that hath an ear, let him hear what *the Spirit* saith unto the churches" (Rev. 2:7, 11, 17, 29; 3:6, 13, 22). As each Person refers us to the teaching of the other, so in like manner does each in turn consummate the ministry of the other. Christ's words and works were not his own, but his Father's: "The words which I speak unto you I speak not of myself: but the Father that dwelleth in me, he doeth the works" (John 14:10). The Spirit's teaching and communications are not his own, but Christ's: "Howbeit when he the Spirit of truth is come, he will guide you into all truth; for he shall not speak of himself; but whatsoever he shall hear that shall he speak; and he will show you things to come" (John 16:13); "He shall glorify me: for he shall receive of mine and show it unto you" (John 16:14).

This order in the ministries of the Persons of the Godhead is so fixed and eternal that we find it distinctly foreshadowed even in the typical teaching of the Old Testament. Many speak slightingly of the types, but they are as accurate as mathematics; they fix the sequence of events in redemption as rigidly as the order of sunrise and noontide is fixed in the heavens. Nowhere in tabernacle or in temple, shall we ever find the laver placed before the altar. The altar is Calvary and the laver is Pentecost; one stands for the sacrificial blood, the other for the sanctifying Spirit. If any high priest were ignorantly to approach the brazen laver without first having come to the brazen altar, we might expect a rebuking voice to be heard from heaven: "Not yet the washing of water"; and such a saying would signify exactly the same as: "Not yet the Holy Spirit."

Again, when the leper was to be cleansed, observe that the blood was to be put upon the tip of his right ear, the thumb of his right hand, and the great toe of his right foot; and then the oil was to be put upon the right ear, the right thumb, and the right foot—the oil upon the blood of the trespass offering (Lev. 14). Never, we venture to say, in all the manifold repetitions of this Divine ceremony, was this order once inverted, so that the oil was first applied, and then the blood. Which means, interpreting type into antitype, that it was impossible that Pentecost could have preceded Calvary, or that the outpouring of the Spirit should have anticipated the shedding of the blood.

Then let us reflect, that not only the order of these two great events of redemption was fixed from the beginning, but their dates were marked in the calendar of typical time. The slaying of the paschal lamb told to generation after generation, though they knew it not, the day of the year and week on which Christ our Passover should be sacrificed for us. The presentation of the wave sheaf before the Lord, "on the morrow after the Sabbath" had for long centuries fixed the time of our Lord's resurrection on the first day of the week. And the command to "count from the morrow after the Sabbath, from the day that ye brought the sheaf of the wave offering, *seven Sabbaths*" (see Lev. 23 for these references), determined the day of Pentecost as the time of the descent of the Spirit. We sometimes think of the disciples waiting for an indefinite period in that upper room for the fulfillment of the promise of the Father; but the time had been fixed not only with God in eternity, but in the calendar of the Jewish ritual upon earth. They tarried in prayer for ten days, simply because after the forty days of the Lord's sojourn on earth subsequent to his resurrection, ten days remained of the "seven Sabbaths" period.

To sum up what we are saying: The Spirit of God is the successor of the Son of God in his official ministry on earth. Until Christ's earthly work for his church had been finished, the Spirit's work in this world could not properly begin. The office of the Holy Spirit is to communicate Christ to us—Christ in his entirety. However perfectly the photographer's plate has been prepared, there can be no picture until his subject steps into his place and stands before him. Our Savior's redemptive work was not completed when he died on the cross, or when he rose from the dead, or even when he ascended from the brow of Olivet. Not until he sat down in his Father's throne, summing up all his ministry in himself—"I am he that liveth and was dead; and behold I am alive for evermore" (Rev. 1:18)—did the full Christ stand ready to be communicated to his church.[2] By the first Adam's sin, God's communion with man through the Holy Spirit was broken, and their union ruptured. When the second Adam came up from his cross and resurrection, and took his place at God's right hand, there was a restoration of this broken fellowship.

Very beautiful are the words of our risen Lord as bearing on this point: "I ascend to my Father and your Father, to my God and your God" (John 20:17).[3] The place which the Divine Son had won for himself in the Father's heart, he had won for us also. All of acceptance and standing and privilege which was now his, was ours too, by redemptive right; and the Holy Spirit is sent down to confirm and realize to us what he had won for us. Without the expiatory work of Christ for us, the sanctifying work of the Spirit in us would have been impossible; and on the other hand, without the work of the Spirit within us, the work of Christ for us would have been without avail.

"And when the day of Pentecost was fully come" (Acts 2:1). What these words mean historically, typically, and doctrinally, we are now prepared to see. The true wave sheaf had been presented in the temple on high. Christ the first-fruits, brought from the grave on "the morrow after the Sabbath," or the first day of the week, now stands before God accepted on our behalf; the seven Sabbaths from the resurrection day have been counted, and Pentecost has come. Then suddenly, to those who were "all of one accord in one place . . . there came a sound from heaven as of a rushing mighty wind, and it filled all the house where they were sitting, and there appeared unto them cloven tongues, like as of fire, and sat upon each of them, and they were all filled with the Holy Spirit" (Acts 2:1-2).

As the manger of Bethlehem was the cradle of the Son of God, so was the upper room the cradle of the Spirit of God. As the advent of "the Holy Child" was a testimony that God had "visited and redeemed his people" so was the coming of the Holy Spirit. The fact that the Comforter is here, is proof that the Advocate is there in the presence of the Father. Boldly Peter and the other apostles now confront the rulers with their testimony, "Whom ye slew and hanged on a tree. Him hath God exalted with his right hand to be a prince and a Savior, to give repentance to Israel and forgiveness of sins; and we are his witnesses of these things; and so also is the Holy Spirit, whom God hath given to them that obey him" (Acts 5:30-32).

As the sound of the golden bells upon the high priest's garments within the Holiest gave evidence that he was alive, so the sound of the Holy Spirit, proceeding from heaven and heard in that upper chamber, was an incontestable witness that the great High Priest whom they had just seen passing through the cloud-curtain, entering within the veil, was still living for them in the presence of the Father. Thus has the *dies natalis,* the birthday of the Holy Spirit, come.

Source for Chapter 9: A. J. Gordon, *The Ministry of the Spirit* (Philadelphia: American Baptist Publication Society, 1896), 18-32.

CHAPTER 10

The Conviction of the Spirit

The Comforter in every part of his threefold work glorifies Christ. In convincing of sin he convinces us of the sin of not believing on Christ. In convincing us of righteousness, he convinces us of the righteousness of Christ, of that righteousness which was made manifest in Christ going to the Father, and which he received to bestow on all such as should believe in him. And lastly, in convincing of judgment, he convinces us that the prince of the world was judged in the life and by the death of Christ. Thus throughout, Christ is glorified; and that which the Comforter shows to us relates in all its parts to the life and work of the incarnate Son of God.
—Julius Charles Hare (1795-1855)

A nd when he is come he will convict the world in respect of sin, and of righteousness, and of judgment" (John 16:8 RV).

It is too large a conclusion which many seem to draw from these words, that since the day of Pentecost the Spirit has been universally diffused in the world, touching hearts everywhere, among Christians and heathen, among the evangelized and the unevangelized alike, and awakening in them a sense of sin. Does not our Lord say in this same discourse concerning the Comforter: " Whom the world cannot receive, because it seeth him not neither knoweth him"? (Jn. 14:17) With these words should be associated the limitation which Jesus makes in the gift of the Paraclete: "If I depart I will send him unto you" (John 16:7).

Christ's disciples were to be the recipients and distributors of the Holy Spirit, and his church the mediator between the Spirit and the world. "And when he is come [to you], he will reprove the world."

And to complete the exposition, we may connect this promise with the Great Commission, "Go ye into all the world and preach the gospel to every creature" (Mark 16:15), and conclude that when the Lord sends his messengers into the world, the Spirit of truth goes with them, witnessing to the message which they bear, convincing of the sin which they reprove, and revealing the righteousness which they proclaim. We are not clear to affirm that the conviction of the Spirit here promised goes beyond the church's evangelizing, though there is every reason to believe that it invariably accompanies the faithful preaching of the Word.

It will help us then to a clear conception of the subject, if we consider the Spirit of truth as sent *unto the church,* testifying *of Christ,* and bringing conviction *to the world.* As there is a threefold work of Christ as prophet, priest, and king, so there is a threefold conviction of the Spirit answering thereto: "And he, when he is come, will convict the world in respect of sin and of righteousness and of judgment; of sin, because they believe not on me; of righteousness, because I go to the Father and ye behold me no more; of judgment, because the prince of this world hath been judged." (John 16:8-12). It is concerning the testimony of Christ as he spoke to men in the days of his flesh, and concerning the work of Christ now carried on in his intercession at God's right hand, and concerning the sentence of Christ when he shall come again to be our judge, that this witness of the Spirit has to do.

"He shall convince the world of sin." Why is he needed for this conviction since conscience is present in every human breast, and is doing its work so faithfully? We reply: Conscience is the witness to the law; the Spirit is the witness to grace. Conscience brings legal conviction; the Spirit brings evangelical conviction. The one begets a conviction unto despair, the other a conviction unto hope.

"Of sin, because they believe not on me," describes the ground of the Holy Spirit's conviction. The entrance of Christ into the world rendered possible a sin before unknown: "If I had not come and spoken unto them, they had not had sin; but now they have no cloak for their sin" (John 15:22).

Evil seems to have required the presence of incarnate goodness, in order to reveal its fullest manifestation. Hence the deep significance of the prophecy spoken over the cradle of Jesus: "Behold this child is set for the fall and rising again of many in Israel; and for a sign which shall be spoken against, that the thoughts of many hearts may be revealed" (Luke 2:34-35). All the most hideous sins of human nature came out during the betrayal and trial and passion of our Lord. In that "hour and power of darkness" (Luke 22:53) these sins seem indeed to have been but imperfectly recognized. But when the day of Pentecost had come, with its awful revealing light of the Spirit of truth, then there was great contrition in Jerusalem—a contrition the sting of which we find in the charge of Peter: "Jesus of Nazareth, whom ye have taken and by wicked hands have crucified and slain" (Acts 2:23). Was not that deep conviction, following the gift of the Spirit, in which three thousand were brought to repentance in a single day, a conviction of sin because they had not believed on Christ?

For our reproof the Holy Spirit presents another side of the same fact, calling us to repentance, not for having taken part in crucifying Christ, but for having refused to take part in Christ-crucified; not for having been guilty of delivering him up to death, but for having refused to believe in him who was "delivered for our offenses and raised again for our justification" (Rom. 4:25). Wherever, by the preaching of the gospel, the fact of Christ having died for the sins of the world is made known, this guilt becomes possible. The sin of disbelieving on Christ is, therefore, the great sin now, because it summarizes all other sins. He bore for us the penalties of the law —and thus our obligation, which was originally to the law, is transferred to him. To refuse faith in him, therefore, is to repudiate the claims of the law which he fulfilled and to repudiate the debt of infinite love which, by his sacrifice, we have incurred.

Nevertheless, the Spirit of truth brings home this sin against the Lord, not to condemn the world, but that the world through him might be saved. In a word, as has been well said, "it is not the sin-question but the Son-question" which we really raise now in preaching the gospel. "Christ having perfectly satisfied God about sin, the question now between God and your heart is: Are you perfectly satisfied with Christ as the alone portion of your soul? Christ has settled every other question to the glory of God." In dealing with the guilty Jews, it was the historical fact which the Holy Spirit urged for their conviction: "Ye denied the Holy One and the Just, and killed the Prince of Life" (Acts 3:14-15). In dealing with us Gentiles, it is rather the theological or evangelical fact: "Christ also hath once suffered for sins, the just for the unjust, that he might bring us to God" (1 Pet. 3:18), and you are condemned that you have not believed on him and confessed him as Savior and Lord.

It is the same sin in the last instance, but viewed upon its reverse side, if we may say it. In the one case it is the guilt of despising and rejecting the Son of God; in the other, it is the guilt of not believing in him who was despised and rejected of men. Yet if submissively yielded to, the Spirit will lead us from this first stage of revelation to the second, since what Andrew Fuller (1754-1815) said of the doctrines of theology is equally true of the convictions of the Spirit, that "they are united together like chain-shot, so that whichever one enters the heart the other must certainly follow."

"Of righteousness, because I go to the Father and ye see me no more." Not until he had been seated in the heavenly places had Christ perfected righteousness for us. As he was "delivered for our offenses and raised again for our justification," so must he be enthroned for our assurance. It is necessary to see Jesus standing at the right hand of God, in order to know ourselves "accepted in the Beloved" (Eph. 1:6). How beautiful the culmination of Isaiah's passion-prophecy wherein, accompanying the promise that "he shall bear the sin of many," is the prediction that "by his knowledge shall my righteous servant justify many" (Isa. 53:11)! But he must be shown to be righteous, in order that he may justify; and this is what his exaltation does. "It was the proof that him whom the world condemned, God justified—that the stone which the builders rejected, God made the Headstone of the corner—that him whom the world denied and lifted up on a cross of shame in the midst of two thieves, God accepted and lifted up in the midst of the throne."[1]

The words "and because ye see me no more," which have perplexed the commentators, seem to us to give the real clue to the meaning of the whole passage. So long as the high priest was within the veil, and unseen, the congregation of Israel could not be sure of their acceptance. Hence the eager anxiety with which they waited his coming out, with the assurance that God had received the propitiation offered on their behalf. Christ, our great High Priest, has entered into the Holy of Holies by his own blood. Until he comes forth again at his second advent, how can we be assured that his sacrifice for us is accepted? We could not be, unless he had sent out one from his presence to make known this fact to us. And this is precisely what he has done in the gift of the Holy Spirit. "Who being the brightness of his glory, and the express image of his person, and upholding all things by the word of his power, when he had by himself purged our sins, he sat down on the right hand of the Majesty on high" (Heb. 1:3). There he will remain throughout the whole duration of the great day of atonement, which extends from ascension to advent. But in order that his church may have immediate assurance of acceptance with the Father, through his Righteous Servant, he sends forth the Paraclete to certify the fact. And the presence of the Spirit in the midst of the church is proof positive of the presence of Jesus in the midst of the throne, as is said by Peter on the day of Pentecost: "Therefore being by the right hand of God exalted, and having received of the Father the promise of the Holy Spirit, he hath shed forth this which ye now see and hear" (Acts 2:33).

Now the Lord's words seem plain to us. Because he ascends to the Father, to be seen no more until his second coming, the Spirit in the meantime comes down to attest his presence and approval with the Father as the perfectly righteous One. How clearly this comes out in Peter's defense before the Council: "The God of our fathers raised up Jesus, whom ye slew and hanged on a tree. Him hath God exalted with his right hand to be a Prince and a Savior, for to give repentance to Israel and forgiveness of sins; and we are witnesses of these things, and so also is the Holy Spirit, whom God hath given to them that obey him" (Acts 5:30-32). Why this twofold witness? The reason is obvious. The disciples could bear testimony to the crucifixion and resurrection of Christ, but not to his enthronement; that event was beyond the knowledge of human vision. So the Holy Spirit, who had been cognizant of that fact in heaven, must be sent down as a joint-witness with the apostles, that thus the whole circle of redemption-truth might be attested. Therein was the promise of Jesus in his last discourse literally fulfilled: "But when the Comforter is come, whom I will send unto you from the Father, even the Spirit of truth which proceedeth from the Father, he shall testify of me; and ye also shall bear witness, because ye have been with me from the beginning" (John 15:26-27).

As we have said, it is not only the enthronement of Christ in righteous approval with the Father that must be certified, but the acceptance of his sacrificial work as a full and satisfying ground of our reconciliation with the Father. And the Spirit proceeding from God is alone competent to bear to us this assurance. Therefore in the Epistle to the Hebrews, after the reiterated statement of our Lord's exaltation at the right hand of God, it is added: "For by one offering he hath perfected forever them that are sanctified, whereof the Holy Spirit is also a witness to us" (Heb. 14-15). In a word, he whom we have known on the cross as "the Lamb of God that taketh away the sins of the world" (John 1:29), must now be known to us on the throne as "the Lord our righteousness" (Jer. 33:16).

But though the angels and the glorified in heaven see Jesus, once crucified, now "made both Lord and Christ" (Acts 2:36), we see him not. Therefore it is written that "no man can say Jesus is Lord, but in the Holy Spirit" (1 Cor. 12:3 RV). So also we are told that "if any man sin we have a Paraclete with the Father, Jesus Christ the righteous" (1 John 2:1 RV); but we can only know Christ as such through that "other Paraclete " sent forth from the Father. It was promised that "when he, the Spirit of truth, is come, he shall not speak from himself; but what things soever he shall hear, these shall he speak" (John 16:13 RV). Hearing the ascriptions of worthiness lifted up to Christ in heaven, and beholding him who was made a little lower than the angels for the suffering of death, now "crowned with glory and honor" (Heb. 2:9), he communicates what he sees and hears to the church on earth. Thus, as he in his earthly life, through his own outshining and self-evidencing perfection, "was justified in the Spirit" (1 Tim. 3:16); so we, recognizing him standing for us in glory, and now "of God made unto us righteousness" (1 Cor. 1:30), are also "justified in the name of the Lord Jesus and by the Spirit of our God" (1 Cor. 6:11).

Thus, though unseen by the church during all the time of his high priestly ministry, our Lord has sent to his church One whose office it is to bear witness to all he is and all he is doing while in heaven. Because that is so, we may have "boldness and access with confidence by the faith of him," and we may come boldly to the throne of grace, "the Holy Spirit this signifying" — what he could not under the old covenant — "that the way into the holiest of all" (Heb. 9:8) has been made manifest.

And yet — strange paradox — in this identical discourse in which Jesus speaks to his disciples of seeing him no more, he says: "Yet a little while and the world seeth me no more, but ye see me; because I live ye shall live also" (John 14:19), in words which by common consent refer to the same time of Christ's continuation within the veil. But it is now by the inward vision, which the world has not, that they are to behold him. And they are to behold him for the world, since Christ said of him: "Whom the world cannot receive, because it seeth him not, neither knoweth him" (John 14:17). And yet it is "to convince the world . . . of sin and of righteousness and of judgment" that the Spirit was to be sent. How shall we make it plain? When the sun retires beyond the horizon at night, the world, our hemisphere, sees him no more; yet the moon sees him, and all night long catches his light and throws it down upon us. So the world sees not Christ in the gracious provisions of redemption which he holds for us in heaven, but through the illumination of the Comforter the church sees him. As it is written: "Eye hath not seen, nor ear heard, neither have entered into the heart of man the things which God hath prepared for them that love him; but God hath revealed them unto us by his Spirit" (1 Cor. 2:9-10). And the church seeing these things, communicates what she sees to the world. Christ is all and in all; and the Spirit receives and reflects him to the world through his people.

> *The moon above, the church below,*
> *A wondrous race they run;*
> *But all their radiance, all their glow,*
> *Each borrows of its sun.*

"Of judgment, because the prince of this world is judged." Here, we believe, is a still further advance in the revelation of the gospel, and

not a retreat to the doctrine of a future judgment, as some would teach. For we repeat our conviction, that in this entire discourse the Holy Spirit is revealed to us as an Evangel of Grace, and not as a sheriff of the Law. Hear the Apostle Peter once more pointing to him who had been raised from the dead and seated in the heavenlies. He says: "By him everyone that believeth is justified from all things from which ye could not be justified by the law of Moses" (Acts 13:39 RV).

Justification, in the evangelical sense, is but another name for judgment prejudged and condemnation ended. In the enthroned Christ every question about sin is answered, and every claim of a violated law is absolutely met. And though there is no abatement in the demands of the Decalogue, yet because "Christ has become the end of the law for righteousness to everyone that believeth" (Rom. 10:4), now "grace reigns through righteousness unto eternal life by Jesus Christ our Lord" (Rom. 5:21). Strange paradox set forth in Isaiah's passion psalm: "By his stripes we are healed" (Isa. 53:5), as though it were told us that sin's smiting had procured sin's remission. And so it is. If the Holy Spirit shows us the wounds of the dying Christ for condemning us, he immediately shows us the wounds of the exalted Christ for comforting us. His glorified body is death's certificate of discharge, the law's receipt in full, assuring us that all the penalties of transgression have been endured, and the Sin-bearer acquitted.

The meaning of this last conviction seems plain therefore: "Of judgment, because the prince of this world is judged." Recall the words of Jesus as he stood face to face with the cross: "Now is the judgment of this world; now shall the prince of this world be cast out" (John 12:31). "The accuser of the brethren" (Rev. 12:10) is at last unsuitable and ejected from court. The death of Christ is the death of death, and of the author of death also. "That through death he might destroy him that hath the power of death, that is, the devil; and deliver them who, through fear of death, were all their lifetime subject to bondage" (Heb. 2:14-15).

If the relation of Satan to our judgment and condemnation is mysterious, this much is clear, from this and several passages, that Christ by his cross has delivered us from his dominion. We must believe that Jesus spoke the literal truth when he said: "Verily, verily, I say unto you, he that heareth my word and believeth him that sent me, hath eternal life, and cometh not unto judgment, but hath passed out of death into life" (John 5:24 RV). On the cross Christ judged sin and acquitted those who believe on him; and in heaven he defends them against every re-arrest by a violated law.

"There is therefore now no condemnation to them that are in Christ Jesus" (Rom. 8:1). Thus the threefold conviction brings the sinner the three stages of Christ's redemptive work, past judgment and past condemnation into eternal acceptance with the Father.

In striking antithesis with all this, we have an instance in the Acts of the threefold conviction of conscience, when Paul before Felix "reasoned of righteousness, and temperance, and the judgment to come (Acts 24:25). Here the sin of a profligate life was laid bare as the apostle discoursed of chastity; the claims of righteousness were vindicated, and the certainty of coming judgment exhibited; and with the only effect that "Felix trembled." So it must ever be under the convictions of conscience—compunction but not peace.

We have also an instructive contrast exhibited in Scripture, between the co-witness of the Spirit and the co-witness of conscience. "The Spirit himself beareth witness that we are the children of God" (Rom. 8:16). Here is the assurance of sonship, with all the Divine inward persuasion of freedom from condemnation which it carries. On the other hand is the conviction of the heathen, who have only the law written in their hearts: "Their conscience bearing witness their thoughts one with another accusing, or else excusing them, in the day when God shall judge the secrets of men" (Rom. 2:15-16). Conscience can "accuse," and how universally it does so, abundant testimony of Christian missionaries shows. And conscience can "excuse," which is the method that guilty thoughts invariably suggest; but conscience cannot justify. Only the Spirit of truth, whom the Father hath sent forth into the world, can do this. The work of the two witnesses may be thus set in contrast:

Conscience Convinces	*The Comforter Convinces*
Of sin committed	of sin committed
Of righteousness impossible	of righteousness imputed
Of judgment impending	of judgment accomplished

Happily these two witnesses may be harmonized, as they are by that atonement which reconciles man to himself, as well as reconciles man to God. Very significantly does the Epistle to the Hebrews, in inviting our approach to God make, as the condition of that approach, the "having our hearts sprinkled from an evil conscience" (Heb. 10:22). As the high priest carried the blood into the Holy of Holies in connection with the old dispensation, so does the Spirit take the blood of Christ into the inner sanctuary of our spirit in the more wondrous economy of the new dispensation, in order that he may "cleanse your conscience from dead works to serve the living God" (Heb. 9:14). Blessed is the man who is thus made at one with himself while made at one with God, so that he can say: "I say the truth in Christ, I lie not, my conscience also bearing me witness in the Holy Spirit" (Rom. 9:11). The believer's conscience dwelling in the Spirit, even as his life is "hid with Christ in God" (Col. 3:3), both having the same mind and bearing the same testimony—this is the end of redemption and this is the victory of the atoning blood.

Source for Chapter 10: A. J. Gordon, *The Ministry of the Spirit* (Philadelphia: American Baptist Publication Society, 1896), 186-202.

CHAPTER 11

The Spirit of Life: Our Regeneration

In his intimate union with his Son, the Holy Spirit is the unique organ which God wills to communicate to man his own life, the supernatural life, the Divine life — that is to say, his holiness, his power, his love, his felicity. To this end the Son works outwardly, the Holy Spirit inwardly.

—G. F. Tophel (1839-1917)

Not until our Lord took his place at God's right hand did he assume his full prerogative as life-giver to us. He was here in the flesh for our death; he took on him our nature that he might in himself crucify our Adam-life and put it away. But when he rose from the dead and sat down on his Father's throne, he became the life-giver to all his mystical body, which is the church.

To talk of being saved by the earthly life of Jesus is to know Christ only "after the flesh" (2 Cor. 5:16). True, the apostle says that "being reconciled" by Christ's death, "much more being reconciled we shall be saved by his life" (Rom. 5:10). But he here refers plainly to his glorified life. And Jesus, looking forward to the time when he should have risen from the dead, says: "Because I live, ye shall live also" (John 14:19). Christ on the throne is really the heart of the church, and every regeneration is a pulse-beat of that heart in souls begotten from above through the Holy Spirit.

The new birth therefore is not a change of nature as it is sometimes defined; it is rather the communication of the Divine nature, and the Holy Spirit is now the Mediator through whom this life is transmitted. If we take our Lord's words to Nicodemus: "Except a man be born again he cannot see the kingdom of God (John 3:3), and press the "again" back to its deepest significance, it becomes very instructive. "Born from above," say some. And very true to fact is this saying. Regeneration is not our natural life carried up to its highest point of attainment, but the Divine life brought down to its lowest point of condescension, even to the heart of fallen man. John, in speaking of Jesus as the life-giver, calls him "he that cometh from above" (3:31). And Jesus, in speaking to the degenerate sons of Abraham, says: "Ye are from beneath; I am from above" (John 8:23). It has been the constant dream and delusion of men that they could rise to heaven by the development and improvement of their natural life. Jesus by one stroke of revelation destroys this hope, telling his hearer that unless he has been begotten of God who is above as truly as he has been begotten of his father on earth, he cannot see the kingdom of God.

Others make these words of our Lord signify "born from the beginning." There must be a resumption of life *de novo,* a return to the original source and fountain of being. To find this it is not enough that we go back to the creation-beginning revealed in Genesis; we must return to the precreation-beginning revealed in John, the book of re-genesis. In the opening of Genesis we find Adam created holy, now fallen through temptation, his face averted from God and leading the whole human race after him into sin and death. In the opening of the Gospel of John we find the Son of God in holy fellowship with the Father. "In the beginning was the Word, and the Word was *toward* God" —not merely proceeding from God, but tending toward God by eternal communion.

Conversion restores man to this lost attitude: "Ye turned to God from idols to serve the living and true God" (1 Thess. 1:9). Regeneration restores man to his forfeited life, the unfallen life of the Son of God, the life which has never wavered from steadfast fellowship with the Father. "I give unto them eternal life" (John 10:28), says Jesus. Is eternal life without end? Yes, and just as truly without beginning. It is uncreated being in distinction from all-created being; it is the "I am" life of God in contrast to the "I become" life of all human souls. By spiritual birth we acquire a Divine heredity as truly as by natural birth we acquire a human heredity.

In the condensed antithesis with which our Lord concludes his demand for the new birth, we have both the philosophy and the justification of his doctrine: "That which is born of the flesh is flesh, and that which is born of the Spirit is spirit. Marvel not that I say unto you, Ye must be born anew" (John 3:7 RV). By no process of evolution, however prolonged, can the natural man be developed into the spiritual man. By no process of degeneration can the spiritual man deteriorate into the natural man. These two are from a totally different stock and origin; the one is from beneath, the other is from above. There is but one way through which the relation of sonship can be established, and that is by begetting. That God has created all men does not constitute them his sons in the evangelical sense of that word. The sonship on which the New Testament dwells so constantly is based absolutely and solely on the experience of the new birth, while the doctrine of universal sonship rests either upon a daring denial or a daring assumption—the denial of the universal fall of man through sin, or the assumption of the universal regeneration of man through the Spirit. In either case, the teaching belongs to "another gospel," the recompense of whose preaching is not a beatitude but an anathema.[1]

The contrast between the two lives and the way in which the partnership—the *koinonia*—with the new is effected, is told in that deep saying of Peter: "Whereby he hath granted us his precious and exceeding great promises; that through these ye may become partakers—*koinonoi*—of the Divine nature, having escaped from the corruption which is in the world by lust" (2 Pet. 1:4 RV). Here are the two streams of life contrasted: the corruption in the world through lust; the Divine nature which is in the world through the incarnation. Here is the Adam-life into which we are brought by natural birth; and over against it the Christ-life into which we are brought by spiritual birth. From the one we escape, of the other we partake. The source and issue of the one are briefly summarized: "Lust when it hath conceived bringeth forth sin, and sin when it is finished bringeth forth death" (James 1:15). The Jordan is a fitting symbol of our natural life, rising in a lofty elevation and from pure springs, but plunging steadily down till it pours itself into that Dead Sea from which there is no outlet. To be taken out of this stream and to be brought into the life which flows from the heart of God is man's only hope of salvation. And the method of effecting this transition is plainly stated, "through these," or by means of the precious and exceeding great promises.

As in grafting, the old and degenerate stock must first be cut off and then the new inserted, so in regeneration we are separated from the flesh and incorporated by the Spirit. And what the scion is in grafting, the word or promise of God is in regeneration. It is the medium through which the Holy Spirit is conveyed, the germ cell in which the Divine life is enfolded. Hence the emphasis which is put in Scripture upon the appropriation of Divine truth. We are told that "of his own will begat he us *with the word of truth*" (James 1:18). " Having been begotten again, not of corruptible seed but of incorruptible, *through the word of God,* which liveth and abideth" (1 Pet. 1:23).

Very deep and significant, therefore, is the saying of Jesus in respect to the regenerating power of his words, in the sixth chapter of the Gospel of John. He emphasizes the contrariety between the two natures, the human and the Divine, saying: "It is the Spirit that quickeneth, the flesh profiteth nothing." And then he adds: "The words which I have spoken unto you are spirit and life." As God in creation breathed into man the breath of life and he became a living soul, so the Lord Jesus by the word of his mouth, which is the breath of life, recreates man and makes him alive unto God. And not life only, but likeness as well, is thus imparted. "So God created man in his own image; in the image of God created he him" (Gen. 1:27), is the simple story of the origin of an innocent race. Then follows the temptation and the fall, and then the story of the descent of a ruined humanity: "And Adam . . . begat a son in his own likeness, and after his image" (Gen. 5:3).

And yet how wide the gulf between these two origins. The notion is persistent and incurable in the human heart, that whatever variation there may have been from the original type, education and training can reshape the likeness of Adam to the likeness of God. "As the twig is bent the tree is inclined," says the popular proverb. True, but though a crooked sapling may be developed into the upright oak, no bending or manipulation can ever so change the species of the tree as to enable men to gather grapes of thorns or figs of thistles. Here again the dualism of Jesus Christ's teaching is distinctly recognized. "A good tree cannot bring forth evil fruit, neither can a corrupt tree bring forth good fruit" (Luke 6:43). And what is the remedy for a corrupt tree? The cutting off of the old and the bringing in of a new scion and stock. The life of God can alone beget the likeness of God; the Divine type is wrapped up in the same germ which holds the Divine nature. Therefore in regeneration we are said to have "put on the new man who is renewed in knowledge after the image of him that created him" (Col. 3:10), and "which after God hath been created in true holiness" (Eph. 4:24).

In a word, the lost image of God is not re-stamped upon us, but renewed within us. Christ our life was "begotten of the Holy Spirit" (Luke 1:35), and he became the fount and origin of life henceforth for all his church. This communication of the Divine life from Christ to the soul through the Holy Spirit is a hidden transaction, but so great in its significance and issues that one has well called it "the greatest of all miracles."

As in the origin of our natural life we are made in secret and curiously wrought, much more in our spiritual. But the issue has to do with the farthest eternity. "As when the Lord was born the world still went on its old way, little conscious that one had come who should one day change and rule all things, so when the new man is framed within, the old life for a while goes on much as before: the daily calling, and the earthly cares, and too often old lusts and habits also, still engross us; a worldly eye sees little new, while yet the life which shall live forever has been quickened within and a new man been formed who shall inherit all."[2]

Source for Chapter 11: A. J. Gordon, *The Ministry of the Spirit* (Philadelphia: American Baptist Publication Society, 1896), 100-107.

CHAPTER 12

Regeneration and Renewal

By regeneration we understand the commencement of the life of God in the soul of man; the beginning of that which had not an existence before; by renewal, the invigoration of that which has been begun, the sustentation of a life already possessed. . . . In the washing of regeneration the new life commences. Having begun, it needs to be supported and preserved. This is effected by the renewing of the Holy Ghost, the flowing into the soul through the supply of the Spirit of Jesus Christ of the varied gifts of the Divine Agent by whom the life itself was imparted at first.

—Thomas Binney (1798-1874)

R egeneration and renewal are related to each other as the planting of the tree is related to its growth. It is very necessary that at the outset we should have a clear conception of what regeneration is. In the manuals of theology we sometimes find it described as "a change of nature." But we must take respectful exception to this definition. For by nature must be meant, of course, human nature; and by the expression "change of nature," it is implied that the natural heart can be so transformed and bettered, that it can bring forth the fruits of righteousness and true holiness. Against this presumption the Word of God enters its solemn and emphatic caveat—"Because the carnal mind is enmity against God: for it is not subject to the law of God, neither indeed call be" (Rom. 8:7).

We hold that the true definition of regeneration is, that it is "the communication of the Divine Nature to man by the operation of the Holy Spirit, through the Word." So writes the Apostle Peter: "Whereby are given unto us exceeding great and precious promises;

that by these we might be partakers of the Divine nature, having escaped the corruption that is in the world through lust" (2 Pet. 1:4). As Christ was made partaker of human nature by his incarnation, that so he might enter into truest fellowship with us, we are made partakers of the Divine Nature by regeneration, that we may enter into truest fellowship with God. That great saying of the Son of God which is so often repeated in the Gospel and Epistles of John, "He that believeth on Me hath eternal life" (e.g., John 6:54; 1 John 2:25), can convey to us only this idea when rightly understood. The eternal life is not our natural life prolonged into endless duration. It is the Divine life imparted to us—the very life of very God communicated to the human soul, and bringing forth there its own proper fruit.

Seeing this point clearly, we can readily understand the process and method of spiritual growth that it consists in the constant mortification of the natural man, and the constant renewal of the spiritual man. We can best illustrate this by using the figure of grafting, which the Scriptures several times employ. Here is a gnarly tree, which bears only sour and stunted fruit. From some rich and perfect stock a scion is brought, which is incorporated into a branch of this tree. Now, the husbandman's efforts are directed, not to the culture and improvement of the old stock, but to the development of the new. Instead of seeking to make the original branches better, he cuts them off, here and there, that the sap and vitality which they are wasting in the production of worthless fruit may go to that which is approved and excellent. Here is the philosophy of spiritual culture: "Put off the old man with his deeds" (Col. 3:9); "the inward man is renewed day by day" (2 Cor. 4:16).

Believing that vigilant and serious attention to spiritual culture is now especially demanded, if we are to cope with the powerful enemies which confront us, let us search for the secret of this Divine renewal.

"Day by day" our inward man is renewed. "Give us day by day our daily bread" (Luke 11:3), is the prayer which the Savior taught us to pray. And yet he said, "It is written that man shall not live by bread alone, but by every word that proceedeth out of the mouth of God" (Matt. 4:4). The bread of the Word is that which we must feed upon if we would enjoy a daily increase in the life of God. It is a trite admonition, but nonetheless true and vital: Divine growth must follow the development of the Divine birth. If we were "begotten by the word of Truth" (James 1:18), we must be daily renewed from the same element.

Too few really credit the power of the Word in building up holy character, and, therefore, too few make diligent practice of the process. Can we think it possible that the food on our tables should be so transmuted in nature's laboratory that it should reappear, now in the stalwart muscle of the blacksmith's arm, and now in the fine texture of the poet's brain? And let it not seem incredible that the Word of God, daily received and inwardly assimilated, can reappear in every kind of spiritual power and holy efficiency. Stephen Grellet (1773-1855), waking up from his early sacramental training, saw the washerwomen one day at their tasks; they were washing linen. He says:

> I wondered to see what beating and pounding there was upon it, and how beautifully white it came out of their hands. I was told I could not enter God's kingdom until I underwent such an operation; that unless I was thus washed and made white, I could have no part in the dear Son of God. For weeks I was absorbed in the consideration of the subject—the washing of regeneration. I had never heard such things before, and I greatly wondered that, having been baptized with water, and having also received what they call the sacrament of confirmation, I should have to pass through such a purification." Just as it was in the beginning, we see, "How shall ye believe if I tell you of heavenly things?"[1]

But by-and-by this mystery is solved, by being wrought out in a living personal experience, and the regeneration of the Spirit is followed by a long life of eager and humble feeding on the Spirit and the Word of God. And now appears a greater mystery. By a strange and subtle power the hearts of kings and emperors are made to open to this saintly preacher, while they listen entranced as he unfolds to them the mysteries of the kingdom of heaven, and pleads the claims of Divine Love. Popes and cardinals, priests and nuns, give ear; their hearts melt, and their eyes flow with tears, while they confess that they never heard it on this wise before. Here is a life which maintained such communion with God, that there was far more of heaven than of earth in it. Let us see in it a living testimony of what the Holy Spirit and the Holy Word can effect when wrought into living Christian character.

We are touching a most vital point now. Physiology shows us how inevitably the food on which one subsists determines the texture of his flesh. Can the daily newspaper, the light romance, and the secular magazine, build up the fiber and tissue of a true spiritual character? We are not putting any surly prohibition on these things; but when we think of the place which they hold in modern society, and with how many Christians they constitute the larger share of the daily reading, there is suggested a very serious theme for reflection. As the solemn necessity is laid upon the sinner of choosing between Christ and the world, so is the choice pressed upon the Christian between the Bible and secular literature—that is, the choice as to which shall hold the supreme place. "Blessed are they that hunger and thirst after righteousness" (Matt. 5:6). Ah! how quickly a day's bodily languor and lack of appetite is noted and attended to. But how many days have we known in which there has been no relish for the Word of God, no deep, inward craving after that meat which the world knows not of. And have we been so alarmed at this symptom that we have made haste at once to seek its cure?

The fact of the Scriptures furnishing nutriment and upbuilding to the soul, is the most real experience of which we have knowledge. None of us "by taking thought can add one cubit unto his stature" (Matt. 6:27). But how many, by taking in God's great thoughts, feeding on them and inwardly digesting them, have added vastly to their spiritual stature. We have noticed especially, in the lives of Christians, how some long-neglected but freshly-revived truth has marvelously quickened and built up the soul. Its newness has created a strong relish in the believer, and so imparted a mighty impulse to his spiritual growth. How true this has been of such doctrines as those of "Justification by Faith," "The Witness of the Spirit," and the "Coming of the Lord." The revival of these doctrines has constituted distinct eras of reformation in the church, but previously, also, marked eras of renewal in the individual soul. We may take the last-mentioned as the one most recently revived. The biographer of Hewitson says of him: "He not only believed in the speedy appearing, but loved it, waited for it, watched for it. So mighty a motive power did it become that he ever used to speak of it afterward as bringing with it a kind of *second conversion.*" Yes, and how many Christians of our day know what this means! Such is the vivifying power of truth; so does it come in to repair the waste in our spiritual life, to build up new tissue, and to put new blood into our heavenly man.

The same may be said of prayer and meditation. They have mighty renewing power. They quicken our life, and multiply within us the joy of the Lord, which is our strength. In these days, when the closet has become so contracted and the church so expanded; when Christians have learned to find their edification so largely in the public services: in the music, and art, and eloquence of the sanctuary, and so little in the still hour of communion, it is quite hard to believe that the greatest enjoyment is possible in solitude with God. We read of Columbkille (521-597) bidding farewell to his hermit's cell and homely fare to take the honors and advantages of the bishopric of Iona, yet exclaiming tearfully: "Farewell, Arran of my heart! Paradise is with thee; the garden of God is within sound of thy bells." And as we read this we say, indeed, "This is monkish sentimentalism."

But when we find sober Protestant saints like the one just quoted, Hewitson, writing: "Communion with Christ is the only source of satisfaction, the only source of lasting joy. I have enjoyed more even this morning from beholding the loveliness of the glory of Christ, as revealed to me by the Spirit, than I have done from the world during the whole of my life." Or, to rise to a still more incredible altitude, what if we listen to that mighty interceder with God, John Welch, of Scotland (1570-1622), crying in one of his seasons of rapt communion, "O Lord, hold Thy hand; it is enough; Thy servant is a clay vessel, and can contain no more"?

Surely, this is strange language to most of us. But if we turn to the Scriptures of our Lord, we may find a possible key to such alleged experiences, for when we ask our Master why he has revealed such wonderful things concerning our union with him, and our share in the Father's glory, he answers, "These things have I spoken unto you that my joy might remain in you, and that your joy might be full" (John 15:11). And when we ask him why he has given us this wonderful privilege of prayer in his name, he replies, "Ask and ye shall receive, that your joy may be full" (John 16:24). If, at best, we have been able to get only a half measure of this Divine joy, let us not discredit those who have exclaimed, "My cup runneth over. Surely goodness and mercy shall follow me all the days of my life" (Psa. 23:6).

We have spoken of daily renewals, and we are persuaded that no real growth and development in Christian life is possible without these. There is still another kind of renewing to which we would call attention: "The times of refreshing: from the presence of the Lord" (Acts 3:19), which the Scriptures promise, hold out a very blessed and assuring hope. This expression, of course, has literal reference to the return of the Lord from glory, and his joyful reunion with his church. But there are even now seasons of extraordinary communion with the Lord, when, through the Holy Spirit, he is pleased to manifest himself to the soul in such exceptional power that they may be truly called "times of refreshing."

We find records of these in the lives of almost all devoted saints. As nature has its annual as well as its diurnal renewals, when the sun returns in springtide blessing and quickening, so has grace its special times of revival. Then it is that the Heavenly Bridegroom visits the soul, by the Holy Spirit, speaking in most tender accents: "Rise up, my love, my fair one, and come away. For lo, the winter is past, the rain is over and gone. The flowers appear on the earth; the time of the singing of birds is come, and the voice of the turtle is heard in the land. The fig tree putteth forth her green figs, and the vines with the tender grapes give a good smell. Arise, my love, my fair one, and come away" (Sg. Sol. 2:11-13). Ah! how often have the poetic strains of this Song of Solomon been translated into the real prose of living, practical experience. The chill of winter has settled over the church; instead of melting penitence, the tears of other days have frozen into icicles, and are hanging about the sanctuary—cold and glittering formalities taking the place of that holy tenderness which pleads with God "with strong crying" (Heb. 5:7), and warns men "night and day with tears" (Acts 20:31).

What servant of God has not had sorrowful experiences of this condition of things? Then it is that pastors and brethren should seek for a special refreshing from the Lord's presence. The ordinary tenor of spiritual life will not answer now. The power of God must be laid hold of—special power for special weakness and need. And "blessed be the God and Father of our Lord Jesus Christ, who hath begotten us again unto a lively hope by the resurrection of Jesus Christ from the dead" (1 Pet. 1:3), that he can renew what he has begotten, and restore the joy of his salvation to those who have backslidden into the joy of this world. Christmas Evans (1766-1838), the fervent Welsh preacher, has left us the record of a most gracious visitation of this kind:

I was weary of a cold heart toward Christ and His sacrifice and the work of His Spirit; of a cold heart in the pulpit, in secret prayer, and in the study. For fifteen years previously I had felt my heart burning within me, as if going to Emmaus with Jesus. On a day ever to be remembered by me, as I was going from Dolgelley to Machynlleth, and climbing up toward Cadair Idris, I considered it incumbent on me to pray, however hard I felt my heart, and however worldly the frame of my spirit was. Having began in the name of Jesus, I soon felt, as it were, the fetters loosening, and the old hardness softening, and, as I thought, the mountains of frost and snow dissolving and melting within me. This engendered confidence in my soul in the promise of the Holy Ghost. I felt my whole mind relieved from some great bondage; tears flowed copiously, and I was constrained to cry out for the gracious visits of God, by restoring to my soul the joy of His salvation, and that He would visit the churches in Anglesea that were under my care. I embraced in my supplications all the churches of the saints, and nearly all the ministers of the principality by their names. This struggle lasted for three hours; it rose again and again, like one wave after another, or a high-flowing tide driven by a strong wind, until my nature became faint by weeping and crying. Thus I resigned myself to Christ, body and soul, gifts and labours, all my life—every day and every hour that remained for me; and all my cares I committed to Christ. The road was mountainous and lonely, and I was wholly alone, and suffered no interruption in my wrestling with God. From this time I was led to expect the goodness of God to the churches and to myself. . . . The result was, when I returned home the first thing that arrested my attention was that the Spirit was working also in the brethren in Anglesea, inducing in them a spirit of prayer, especially in two of the deacons, who were particularly importunate that God would visit us in mercy, and render the Word of His grace effectual amongst us for the conversion of sinners.[2]

What is especially to be noticed in this experience is its relation to the church of God. When the ice was melted from his own soul, then he began to plead for all the saints and all the ministers. And, as afterwards appears, at the same time that the Spirit fell on him it was falling on his brothers in distant places. So it is always. God never makes half a providence any more than man makes half a pair of shears. If he fits a preacher to declare his Word, he fits a hearer to receive that Word; if he moves one soul to cry, "What must I do?" He has always moved some other servant of his to direct him what to do.

Let us ponder the story of Paul and Ananias, of Peter and Cornelius, of Philip and the eunuch, if we would observe the mystery of the Spirit—his twofold ministry, to preacher and to hearer, to counselor and to inquirer. And noting this, we shall understand the intimate relationship between the season of renewal in the heart of the individual believer and the time of reviving in the church. If two harp strings are in perfect tune, you cannot smite the one without causing the other to vibrate; and if one Christian is touched and agitated by the Spirit of God, think it not strange that all who are like-minded in the church are moved by the same Divine impulse. Not for ourselves, and that we may enjoy the holy luxury of communion with God, are we to seek for the times of refreshing. If so, doubtless we shall fail of them, for even spiritual blessings we may ask and receive not, if we only ask that we may consume them upon ourselves.

No biography to which we have been introduced seems to us more instructive on this point than that of David Brainerd (1718-1747). From time to time he sought and obtained the holiest intimacies with God, yet never for himself. Trace, line by line, the following remarkable passage from his diary:

> April 19, 1742. I set apart this day for fasting and prayer to God for His grace; especially to prepare me for the work of the ministry, to give me Divine aid and time to send me into His harvest. Accordingly, in the morning I endeavored to plead for the Divine Presence for the day, and not without some life. In the forenoon I felt the power of intercession for precious, immortal souls, for the advancement of the kingdom of my dear Lord and Savior in the world, and, withal, a most sweet resignation and even consolation and joy in the thought of suffering hardships, distresses, and even death itself, in the promotion of it; and had special enlargement in pleading for the enlightening and conversion of the poor heathen. In the afternoon God was with me of a truth. Oh, it was blessed company indeed! God enabled me so to agonize in prayer that I was quite wet with sweat, though in the shade and the cool wind. My soul was drawn out very much for the world; I grasped for multitudes of souls. I think I had more enlargement for sinners than for the children of God, though I felt as if I could spend my life in cries for both. I had great enjoyment in communion with my dear Savior. I think I never in my life felt such an entire weanedness from this world, and so much resigned to God in everything. Oh, that I may always live to and upon my blessed God! Amen, amen.[3]

Here, certainly, is something very high and remote from ordinary experience—this praying one's self into fellowship with Christ's sufferings, and into partnership with his garden sweat. But we are writing now for those who wish to know concerning the highest attainments. Yet what we are especially emphasizing is the relation of these extraordinary experiences to the furtherance of the gospel and the salvation of souls.

He who in thus interceding grasped not for some ecstatic vision or revelation of God, but "for multitudes of souls," gained what he sought, for marvelous power attended his preaching. There were days in which the Spirit of God fell upon those stolid, hard-hearted Indians with such demonstration that scores of them bowed before the preacher like grass before the mower's scythe, so that even the ambassador himself was astonished, and exclaimed, "And there was no day like that before it or after it."

Brainerd had many seasons of this uncommon renewing of his spiritual life through prayer and fasting; and in summing them up, President Jonathan Edwards (1703-1758) records this noteworthy conclusion: "Among all the many days he spent in secret prayer and fasting, of which he gives an account in his diary, there is scarcely an instance of one which was not either attended or soon followed with apparent success, and a remarkable blessing in special influences and consolations of God's Spirit, and very often before the day was ended."

And we may add yet more. The record of these fastings and prayers of Brainerd, and of the power of God which followed, written only for himself, but wisely published by Edwards after his death, has brought rich blessing to the world. William Carey (1761-1834) read it on his shoemaker's bench, and asked, "If God can do such things among the Indians of America, why not among the pagans of India?" Henry Martyn (1781-1812), the thoughtful student in Cambridge, England, read it, and was moved by it to consecrate his life to missionary service in the East. Edward Payson (1783-1827) pondered it, and when twenty-two years of age wrote in his diary: "In reading Mr. Brainerd's life, I seemed to feel a most earnest desire after some portion of his spirit." Considering the vast results which have followed the labors of these servants of God, who shall say that Brainerd has not wrought even more since his death than in his life?[4] And who, looking at the great sum total, can question whether or not it is profitable for one to wait upon the Lord with prayer, and fasting, and intercession, for the renewal of his spiritual strength?

O Holy Spirit, quicken us by Thy mighty power, so that we may, "put off concerning the former conversation the old man, which is corrupt according to the deceitful lusts; and be renewed in the spirit of our mind; and that we may put on the new man, which after God is created in righteousness and true holiness" (Eph. 4:22-24).

Source for Chapter 12: A. J. Gordon, *The Twofold Life* (London: Hodder and Stoughton, 1900), 12-27. Retrieved from: http://www. gordon.edu/page.cfm?iPageID=1805.

CHAPTER 13

The Embodying of the Spirit

But now the Holy Ghost is given more perfectly, for he is no longer present by his operation as of old, but is present with us so to speak, and converses with us in a substantial manner. For it was fitting that, as the Son had conversed with us in the body, the Spirit should also come among us in a bodily manner.

—Gregory Nyssa (335-395)

The church, which is his body" (Eph. 1:22), began its history and development at Pentecost. Believers had been saved, and the influences of the Spirit had been manifested to men in all previous dispensations from Adam to Christ. But now an *ecclesia*, an out-gathering, was to be made to constitute the mystical body of Christ, incorporated into him the Head and indwelt by him through the Holy Spirit.

The definition which we sometimes hear, that a church is "a voluntary association of believers, united together for the purposes of worship and edification" is most inadequate, not to say incorrect. It is no more true than that hands and feet and eyes and ears are voluntarily united in the human body for the purposes of locomotion and work. The church is formed from within; Christ present by the Holy Spirit, regenerating men by the sovereign action of the Spirit, and organizing them into himself as the living center. The Head and the body are therefore one, and predestined to the same history of humiliation and glory. And as they are one in fact, so are they one in name. He whom God anointed and filled with the Holy Spirit is called "the

Christ," and the church, which is his body and fullness, is also called" the Christ." "For as the body is one, and hath many members, and all the members of that one body, being many, are one body, *so also is the Christ*" (1 Cor. 12:12). Here plainly and with wondrous honor the church is named the *Christos*. In commenting upon this fact, Bishop Lancelot Andrews (1555-1626) beautifully says, "Christ is both in heaven and on earth; as he is called the Head of his church, he is in heaven; but in respect of his body which is called *Christ*, he is on earth."

So soon as the Holy Spirit was sent down from heaven this great work of his embodying began, and it is to continue until the number of the elect shall be accomplished, or unto the end of the present dispensation. Christ, if we may say it reverently, became mystically a babe again on the day of Pentecost, and the hundred and twenty were his infantile body, as once more through the Holy Spirit he incarnated himself in his flesh. Now he is growing and increasing in his members, and so will he continue to do "till we all come in the unity of the faith and of the knowledge of the Son of God unto a perfect man, unto the measure of the stature of fullness of Christ" (Eph. 4:13). Then the Christ on earth will be taken up into visible union with the Christ in heaven, and the Head and the body be glorified together.

Observe how the history of the church's formation, as recorded in the Acts, harmonizes with the conception given above. The story of Pentecost culminates in the words, "and the same day there were added about three thousand souls" (Acts 2 : 41). Added to whom? we naturally ask. And the King James translators have answered our question by inserting in italics "to them." But not so speaks the Holy Spirit. And when, a few verses further on in the same chapter, we read: "And the Lord added to the church daily such as should be saved" (Acts 5:47), we need to be reminded that the words "to the church" are spurious. All such glosses and interpolations have only tended to mar the sublime teaching of this first chapter of the Holy Spirit's history. "And believers were the more added *to the Lord*" (Acts 5:14). "And much people were added *unto the Lord*" (Acts 11:24.) This is the language of inspiration—not the mutual union of believers, but their Divine co-uniting with Christ; not voluntary association of Christians, but their sovereign incorporation into the Head and this incorporation effected by the Head through the Holy Spirit. If we ask concerning the way of admission into this Divine *ecclesia*, the teaching of Scripture is explicit: "For in one Spirit were we all baptized into one body" (1 Cor. 12:13). The baptism in water marks the formal introduction of the believer into the church; but this is the symbol, not the substance. For observe the identity of form between the ritual and the spiritual. "I indeed baptize you in water,". . . said John, "but he that cometh after me . . . shall baptize you in the Holy Spirit and in fire" (Matt. 3:11).

As in the one instance the disciple was submerged in the element of water, so in the other he was to be submerged in the element of the Spirit. And thus it was in actual historic fact. The upper room became the Spirit's baptistery, if we may use the figure. His presence "filled all the house where they were sitting. . . . And they were all filled with the Holy Spirit" (Acts 2:2, 4). The baptistery would never need to be refilled, for Pentecost was once and for all, and the Spirit then came to abide in the church perpetually. But each believer throughout the age would need to be *in*filled with that Spirit which dwells in the body of Christ. In other words, it seems clear that the baptism of the Spirit was given once for the whole church, extending from Pentecost to the *Parousia*, the second coming of Christ. "There is one Lord, one faith, one baptism" (Eph. 4:5). As there is one body reaching through the entire dispensation, so there is "one baptism" for that body given on the day of Pentecost. Thus, if we rightly understand the meaning of Scripture it is true, both as to time and as to fact, that "in one Spirit we were all baptized into one body, whether Jews or Greeks, whether bond or free" (1 Cor. 12:13).

The typical foreshadowing, as seen in the church in the wilderness, is very suggestive at this point: "Moreover, brethren, I would not that ye should be ignorant, how that all our fathers were under the cloud and all passed through the sea; and were all baptized into Moses in the cloud and in the sea" (1 Cor. 10:1). Baptized *into* Moses by their passage through the sea, identified with him as their leader, and committed to him in corporate fellowship. Even so were they also baptized into Jehovah, who in the cloud of glory now took his place in the midst of the camp and tabernacled henceforth with them. The type is perfect as all inspired types are. The antitype first appears in Christ our Lord, baptized in water at the Jordan, and then baptized in the Holy Spirit which "descended from heaven like a dove and abode upon him" (Luke 3:22). Then it reoccurred again in the waiting disciples, who beside the baptism of water, which had doubtless already been received, now were baptized "in the Holy Spirit and in fire" (Matt. 3:11). Henceforth they were in the Divine element, as their fathers had been in the wilderness, "not in the flesh but *in the Spirit*" (Rom. 8:9); called "to live according to God *in the Spirit*" (1 Pet. 4:6); to "walk *in the Spirit*" (Gal. 5 : 2 5); "praying always with all prayer and supplication *in the Spirit*" (Eph. 6:18). In a word, on the day of Pentecost the entire body of Christ was baptized into the element and presence of the Holy Spirit as a permanent condition. And though one might object that the body as a whole was not yet in existence, we reply that neither was the complete church in existence when Christ died on Calvary, yet all believers are repeatedly said to have died with him.

To change the figure of baptism for a moment to another which is used synonymously, that of the anointing of the Spirit, we have in Exodus a beautiful typical illustration of our thought. At Aaron's consecration the precious ointment was not only poured upon his head, but ran down in rich profusion upon his body and upon his priestly garments. This fact is taken up by the psalmist when he sings: "Behold how good and pleasant it is for brethren to dwell together in unity. It is like the precious ointment upon the head that ran down upon the beard, even Aaron's beard, that went down to the skirts of his garments" (Psa. 133:1-2). Of our great High Priest we read: "How God anointed Jesus of Nazareth with the Holy Spirit and with power" (Acts 10:38). But it was not for himself alone but also for his brethren that he obtained this holy unction. He received that he might communicate. "Upon whom thou shalt see the Spirit descending and remaining on him, the same is he that baptizeth in the Holy Spirit" (John 1:33) And now we behold our Aaron, our great High Priest, who has passed through the heavens, Jesus the Son of God, standing in the holiest in heaven. "Thou didst love righteousness and didst hate iniquity," is the Divine commendation now passed upon him, "therefore God, thy God, anointed thee with the oil of gladness above thy fellows" (Heb. 1:9). He, the *Christos,* the Anointed, stands above and for the *Christoi,* his anointed brethren, and from him the Head, the unction of the Holy Spirit descended on the day of Pentecost. It was poured in rich profusion upon his mystical body. It has been flowing down ever since, and will continue to do so till the last member shall have been incorporated with himself, and so anointed by the one Spirit into the one body, which is the church.

It is true that in one instance subsequent to Pentecost the baptism in the Holy Spirit is spoken of. When the Spirit fell on the house of Cornelius, Peter is reminded of the word of the Lord, how that he said: "John indeed baptized in water, but ye shall be baptized in the Holy Spirit" (Acts 11:16). This was a great crisis in the history of the church, the opening of the door of faith to the Gentiles, and it would seem that these new subjects of grace now came into participation of an already present Spirit. Yet Pentecost still appears to have been the age-baptism of the church. As Calvary was once for all, so was the visitation of the upper room.

Consider now that, as through the Holy Spirit we become incorporated into the body of Christ, we are in the same way assimilated to the Head of that body, which is Christ. An unsanctified church dishonors the Lord, especially by its incongruity. A noble head, lofty-browed and intellectual, upon a deformed and stunted body, is a pitiable sight. What, to the angels and principalities who gaze evermore upon the face of Jesus, must be the sight of an unholy and misshapen church on earth, standing in that place of honor called "his body."

Photographing in a sentence the ecclesia of the earliest centuries, Professor Adolf Harnack says: "Originally the church was the heavenly bride of Christ, and the abiding place of the Holy Spirit." Let the reader consider how much is involved in this definition. The first and most sacred relation of the body is to the head. Watching for the return of the Bridegroom induces holiness of life and conduct in the bride. And the supreme work of the Spirit is directed to this end, that "He may establish our hearts unblamable in holiness before God our Father, at the coming of our Lord Jesus Christ with all his saints" (1 Thess. 3:13). In accomplishing this end he effects all other and subordinate ends. The glorified Christ manifests himself to man through his body. If there is a perfect correspondence between himself and his members, then there will be a true manifestation of himself to the world.[1] Therefore does the Spirit abide in the body, that the body may be "inChristed," to use an old phrase of the mystics; that is, indwelt by Christ and transfigured into the likeness of Christ. Only thus, as "a chosen generation, a royal priesthood, a holy nation, a peculiar people," can it "shew forth the virtues of him who has called us out of darkness into his marvelous light" (1 Pet. 2:9). And who is the Christ that is thus to be manifested? From the throne he gives us his name: "I am he that liveth and was dead, and behold I am alive for evermore" (Rev. 1:18). Christ in glory is not simply what he is, but what he was and what he is to be. As a tree gathers up into itself all the growth of former years, and contains them in its trunk, so Jesus on the throne is all that he was and is and is to be. In other words, his death is a perpetual fact as well as his life.

And his church is predestined to be like him in this respect, since it not only heads up in him, as the apostle says, that ye "may grow up into him in all things which is the Head, even Christ," but also incarnates itself from him, "from whom the whole body, fitly joined together and compacted by that which every joint supplieth . . . maketh increase of the body" (Eph. 4:16).

If the church will literally manifest Christ, then she must be both a living and a dying church. To this she is committed in the divinely given form of her baptism. "Know ye not that so many of us as were baptized into Jesus Christ were baptized into his death; therefore we were buried with him by baptism into death, that like as Christ was raised up from the dead by the glory of the Father, even so we also should walk in newness of life" (Rom. 6:3-4). And the baptism of the Holy Spirit into which we have been brought is designed to accomplish inwardly and spiritually what the baptism of water foreshadows outwardly and typically: to reproduce in us the living and the dying of our Lord.

First, the living. "For the law of the Spirit of life in Christ Jesus hath made me free from the law of sin and death" (Rom. 8: 2). That is, that which has been hitherto the actuating principle within us—sin and death—is now to be met and mastered by another principle, the law of life, of which the Holy Spirit of God is the author and sustainer. As by our natural spirit we are connected with the first Adam, and made partakers of his fallen nature, so by the Holy Spirit we are now united with the second Adam, and made partakers of his glorified nature. To vivify the body of Christ by maintaining its identity with the risen Head is, in a word, the unceasing work of the Holy Spirit.

Secondly, the dying of our Lord in his members is to be constantly effected by the indwelling Spirit. The church, which is "the fullness of him that filleth all in all" (Eph. 1:23), completes in the world his crucifixion as well as his resurrection. This is certainly Paul's profound thought, when he speaks of filling up "that which is behind of the afflictions of Christ in my flesh, for his body's sake, which is the church" (Col. 1: 24). In other words, the church, as the complement of her Lord, must have a life experience and a death experience running parallel.

It is remarkable how exact is this figure of the body, which is employed to symbolize the church. In the human system life and death are constantly working together. A certain amount of tissue must die every day and be cast out and buried, and a certain amount of new tissue must also be created and nourished daily in the same body. Arrest the death process, and it is just as certain to produce disorder as though you were to arrest the life process. Literally is this true of the corporate body also. The church must die daily in fulfillment of the crucified life of her Head, as well as live daily in the manifestation of his glorified life. This italicized sentence, which we take from a recent book, is worthy to be made a golden text for Christians: *"The church is Christian no more than as it is the organ of the continuous passion of Christ."* To sympathize, in the literal sense of suffering with our sinning and lost humanity, is not only the duty of the church, but the absolutely essential condition to her true manifestation of her Lord. A self-indulgent church disfigures Christ; an avaricious church bears false witness against Christ; a worldly church betrays Christ, and gives him over once more to be mocked and reviled by his enemies.

The resurrection of our Lord is prolonged in his body, as we all see plainly. Every regeneration is a pulse-beat of his throne-life. But too little do we recognize the fact that his crucifixion must be prolonged side by side with his resurrection. "If any man will come after me let him deny himself and take up his cross daily and follow me" (Luke 9:23). The church is called to live a glorified life in communion with her Head, and a crucified life in her contact with the world. And the Holy Spirit dwells evermore in the church to effect this twofold manifestation of Christ. "But God be thanked, that ye have obeyed from the heart that pattern of doctrine to which ye were delivered," writes the apostle (Rom. 6:17). The pattern, as the context shows, is Christ dead and risen. If the church truly lives in the Spirit, he will keep her so pliable that she will obey this Divine mold as the metal conforms to the die in which it is struck. If she yields to the sway of "the spirit that now worketh in the children of disobedience" (Eph. 2:2), she will be stereotyped according to the fashion of the world, and they that look upon her will fail to see Christ in her.

Source for Chapter 13: A. J. Gordon, *The Ministry of the Spirit* (Philadelphia: American Baptist Publication Society, 1896), 52-64.

CHAPTER 14

Conversion and Consecration

I must say that I never have had so close and satisfactory a view of the gospel salvation, as when I have been led to contemplate it in the light of a simple offer on the one side, and a simple acceptance on the other.

—Thomas Chalmers (1780-1847)

Full consecration may in one sense be the act of a moment, and in another the work of a lifetime. It must be complete to be real, and yet, if real, it is always incomplete; a point of rest, and yet a perpetual progression. Suppose you make over a piece of ground to another person. From the moment of giving the title-deed, it is no longer your possession; it is entirely his. But his practical occupation of it may not appear all at once. There may be wasteland which he will take into cultivation only by degrees. . . . Just so it is with our lives. The transaction of, so to speak, making them over to God is definite and complete. But then begins the practical development of consecration.

—Frances Ridley Havergal (1837-1879)

These two facts in our spiritual history seem to us to be often strangely confounded. We make a radical distinction between them. In conversion we receive; in consecration we give; in the one we accept eternal life from God; in the other we offer up ourselves in self-surrender to God; in the one we appropriate the work of Christ done for us, in the other we fulfill the work of the Spirit in us.

Inquirers are not infrequently counseled to give their hearts to Christ, or to consecrate themselves to the Lord. We would not be overly critical with what is well meant. But really this is not the gospel. The good news of grace is that God has given to us eternal life and redemption through his Son, and that in order to be saved the sinner has nothing to do but to accept it. Indeed, why should one be asked to give, when he has nothing acceptable to bring?

"It is more blessed to give than to receive" (Acts 20:35); and the Lord, who is alone worthy, takes this highest beatitude for himself, and puts the whole race of unrenewed sinners into the position of helpless and dependent receivers.[1]

"For God so loved the world, that *he gave* his only-begotten Son" (John 3:16).
"As many as *received* him, to them gave he power to become the sons of God" (John 1:2).
"The *gift* of God is eternal life" (Rom. 6:23).
"Whosoever will, let him *take* the water of life freely" (Rev. 22:7).
"Christ also loved the church, and *gave* himself for it" (Eph. 5:25).
"As ye have therefore *received* Christ Jesus the Lord" (Col. 2:6).

But having received the gift of God and been made a partaker of his converting grace, and then and therefore the Divine obligation for service begins to press upon us. The Lord becomes an asker as soon as we have become recipients "As ye have therefore received Christ Jesus the Lord, so walk ye in him" (Col. 2:6). Let consecration crown conversion, let self-devotion to Christ answer to his self-devotion for you. Has the reader noticed the significant "therefore" in that earnest plea for consecration with which Romans 12 opens? Just previously the question has been asked, "Or who hath first given to him, and it shall be recompensed unto him again?" (Rom. 11:35). Had we first rendered something to God, we might look for a return. But, on the contrary, we have received everything from him—"for of him and through him and to him are all things" (Rom. 11:36). And this is the reason why we should render to him all that we have. "I beseech you, *therefore*, brethren, by the mercies of God, that ye present your bodies a living sacrifice, holy, acceptable unto God, which is your reasonable service" (Rom. 12:1).

One love demands another. If God has shown his love to us by giving his Son to die as a sacrifice for our sins, let us show our love by giving ourselves to live in daily sacrifice for him. "By giving ourselves," we say. Self-sacrifice may be seen in two ways. We may give our possessions, instead of giving ourselves; or we may give ourselves to God's service instead of to God himself. In either case our sacrifice is lame and our consecration lacking. There must be self-surrender to him who surrendered himself for us, before Christ can be "all, and in all." Have we not found persons giving their money to charity, under the idea that their gift would in some way sanctify the giver and make him acceptable to the Lord? But God requires our persons before he asks our purses.

We are to "present our bodies" unto him, and that will carry our possessions. For the body is "the temple of the Holy Spirit" (1 Cor. 6:19), and Jesus tells us that it is the temple that sanctifies the gold, and not the gold that sanctifies the temple. The devotion of self, therefore, must go before devotion of property and possessions. This is the Divine order which the apostle so thankfully recognizes in acknowledging the gifts of the Macedonian Christians. For making mention of the riches of their liberality, he adds, "And this they did, not as we expected, but first gave their own selves to the Lord, and unto us by the will of God" (2 Cor. 8:5). And for this cause he declares that he ministered the gospel of God to the Gentiles, that being renewed by the Spirit, they might be prepared to give in the Spirit, "that the offering up of the Gentiles might be acceptable, being sanctified by the Holy Spirit" (Rom. 15:16). And the opposite idea is equally true, that we must devote ourselves *to the Lord,* not merely to some work for the Lord, which may absorb in itself the interest and zeal which should be bestowed on his Divine person.

Now nothing is clearer than the fact that a Christian gets power from God, just in proportion to the entirety of his self-surrender to God. If we ask how this is, the answer is easy. It is not that God keeps a strictly debt and credit account with the Christian, giving so much grace for so much sacrifice, so much power for so much humility. It is by the action of a necessary law that it comes to pass. We know that, in the human body, the deprivation of anyone of the senses only intensifies the power of those which remain. If, for example, the sight is lost, the touch and taste become thereby much more acute. Exactly so it is between the three factors of our human being—body, soul, and spirit. Whatever either one surrenders is carried over to the credit of the others, and inures to their strength. That is why fasting helps communion—the carnal appetites being denied that the spiritual appetites may be awakened to a more hungry craving. Hence the significance of the plea that we present our *bodies* a living sacrifice. We could have said "bodies and spirits," and many so enlarge the exhortation. But no! Let the body be surrendered up for the enrichment of the soul, fleshly desires repressed, that spiritual desires may be enlarged—the carnal man, in a word, sacrificed to the spiritual.

We have seen this significant device on an ancient seal—the effigy of a burning candle, and underneath it the superscription, *"I give light by being myself consumed."* This is the true symbol of Christian devotion—giving out light by giving up our lives to him who loved us—the zeal of God's house consuming us while we furnish Divine illumination to the world.

And this leads us to urge what we believe to be all-important to this whole subject—that we should make our consecration a definite, final, and irrevocable event in our spiritual history. It is not enough for us to hear one say that he believes in Jesus Christ; we lack a decisive and confessed act of acceptance. And likewise we are not satisfied to urge upon our readers a consecrated life merely; we wish to insist on the value and power of a solemn and definite and overshadowing act of consecration. Let it be made with the utmost deliberation, and after the most prayerful self-examination. Let the seal of God's acceptance of it be most carefully sought; let it be final, in the sense of being irrevocable, but initiatory in the sense of being introductory to a new life—a life that belongs, henceforth, utterly to God, to be lived where he would have it lived, to be employed as he would have it employed, to be finished when he would have it finished. Oh, who is sufficient for such an engagement! But many have made it, and we find in them a living demonstration of its value.

In the spiritual history of George Whitefield(1714-1770) we have a striking example of such definite and wholehearted consecration. With John Wesley (1703-1791) and Charles Wesley (1707-1788) in the "Holy Club" of Oxford, he had sought with prolonged prayer and self-mortification for a deeper work of the Spirit in his heart. Whole days he had spent in wrestling with God for the blessing. He found what he sought, and, at his ordination, was made ready to give himself unreservedly to God.

He thus speaks of this experience:

"When the Bishop laid his hands upon my head, if my evil heart doth not deceive me, I offered up my whole spirit, soul, and body, to the service of God's sanctuary. Let come what will, life or death, depth or height, I shall henceforth live like one who this day, in the presence of men and angels, took the holy sacrament upon the profession of being inwardly moved by the Holy Ghost to take upon me that ministration in the church. . . . I can call heaven and earth to witness that, when the Bishop laid his hand upon me, I gave myself up, to be a martyr for Him who hung upon the cross for me. Known unto Him are all future events and contingencies. I have thrown myself blindfolded, and I trust without reserve, into His almighty hands."[2]

Such was his vow of self-devotion to God, and it must be acknowledged that his whole subsequent life attested its sincerity. And in what life, we may ask, has the power of consecration been more signally displayed? We speak not merely of his seraphic eloquence, but of the immediate saving results of his preaching. We judge that other preachers have produced as powerful impression upon congregations—Jacques Bossuet (1627-1704), Robert Hall (1764-1831), Thomas Chalmers (1780-1847), and many more. But that lightning-like penetration of the spoken word which rends men's hearts, and lays bare their sins, and brings out the tears of penitence—here is the test of power. And from the very first sermon of Whitefield, when fifteen were driven to an agony of conviction, to the last, this was the uniform result of his ministry.

John Newton (1725-1807) records of Whitefield that in a single week he received no less than a thousand letters from those distressed in conscience under his preaching. Surely this was not the fruit of his "graceful oratory," which Benjamin Franklin and Chesterfield so much admired, but of that power from on high which is promised to those who are ready to tarry in Jerusalem until they be endued with it. How significant the apostle's description of effective preaching! "For our gospel came not unto you in word only, but also in power and in the Holy Spirit, and in much assurance" (1 Thess. 1:5).

Words, kindled and glowing with the fire of intellectual excitement, can rouse and thrill and overpower, till the effect seems something quite supernatural. But intellect and the Holy Spirit must not be confounded. The highest reach of genius comes far short of the lowest degree of inspiration. To electrify a hearer is one thing; to bring a hearer prostrate at the feet of Jesus is quite another. The one effect is "in word only"; the other is "in power and in the Holy Spirit." And the latter result we have often seen accomplished through the plainest speech, and by the humblest instruments. But how subtle and elusive is the "power"! He who desires it for the sake of being great, can no more have it than Simon Magus could buy it with money. How many a servant of God has quenched the Spirit in his inordinate desire to shine; how often has the soul winner gone out of the pulpit because the orator has come in and filled the entire foreground with himself. So then, the orator cannot teach us the secret. He can help us in word only. The consecration, by which we put ourselves utterly into the hands of God, to be subject to his will and to be swayed by his Spirit, is the only true pathway to power.

Of course as there are diversities of gifts from the same Spirit, so the manifestations of spiritual energy will be widely various. We will select an example which stands in total contrast from that just considered. Stephen Grellet, the saintly Quaker, was endued with extraordinary power as a witness for Christ. "Over two hemispheres he bore a testimony adapted, with marvelous wisdom, alike to dwellers in palaces and in slaves' huts, to the inmates of ecclesiastical mansions and common jails, and yet nonetheless suited to the periodic meetings of Friends, and to large assemblies of Roman Catholics and Protestants, in Europe and America."[3] His was preeminently a ministry of love. The word in the mouth of Whitefield was a sharp two-edged sword, piercing and wounding unto life eternal. From the lips of Grellet, that word distilled like the dew, even "as the dew of Hermon that descended upon the mountains of Zion; for there the Lord commanded the blessing, even life for evermore" (Psa. 133:3).

If we ask whence this strange enchantment which he threw over human hearts so that they opened to his words irresistibly, in spite of prejudice and stern tradition, the answer is easily found. It was the love of Christ acting divinely through one who had given himself up to be led of God, and who, as he wrote on the last page of his journal, had learned the habit of "keeping a single eye to the putting forth of the Divine Spirit." This good man had had his Pentecost — blessed and never to be forgotten — from which he dated a new enduement of power. Referring to the time and place of this transaction he says:

"There the Lord was pleased, in an humbling and memorable manner, to visit me again and to comfort me. I had gone into the woods, which are there mostly of very lofty and large pines, and my mind being inwardly retired before the Lord, He was pleased so to reveal His love to me, through His blessed Son, my Savior, that many fears and doubts were at that time removed, my soul's wounds were healed, my mourning was turned into joy. He clothed me with the garment of praise, instead of the spirit of heaviness, and He strengthened me to offer up myself again freely to Him and to His service for my whole life. Walk, O my soul, in that path which thy blessed Master has trodden before thee and has consecrated for thee. Be willing also to die to thyself, that thou mayest live through faith in Him."

Here is a life which constituted a kind of living exegesis of that text, "speaking the truth in love" (Eph. 4:15). And, accustomed as we are to measure power by outward demonstration, it furnishes a most instructive lesson for us. Two chemical elements which are very mild and innocuous in themselves, often have prodigious energy when combined. So it is of love and truth. Those who preach love alone are often the weakest and most ineffective witnesses for Christ. Those who preach the truth alone, not infrequently demonstrate the feebleness of a soulless orthodoxy. But the truth in love is vital, penetrating, and has the dynamic force which we seek. See how Paul, the apostle of truth, and John, the apostle of love, match and complement each other on this point. "Speaking the truth in love," writes the one,

"Unto the well beloved Gaius, whom I love in the truth" (3 John 1:1). writes the other.

Love furnishing the atmosphere of truth, the medium through which it shines, and by which it is transmitted; and truth lending its gravity and restraint to love, and so preventing it from flying off into a reckless and indiscriminate tolerance, this is the combination which gives true power. "Grace is poured into thy lips; therefore God hath blessed thee for ever" (Psa. 45:2). Grace that wings the gentle speech; grace that imparts the heavenly unction; grace that is invested with the irresistible might of weakness—this is the true secret of Divine efficiency—and yet only half the secret. "Grace and truth came by Jesus Christ" (John 1:17). Oh, for a conformity to Christ and a nonconformity to the world, that shall enable us to grasp both these gifts! Then the highway of power will be open before us, and we may realize the beautiful ideal of the faithful witness: "He had eyes lifted up to heaven, the best of books was in his hand, then law of truth was written upon his lips, the world was behind his back. He stood as if he pleaded with men; and a crown of glory did hang over his head."[4]

Let it not be presumed, however, that the way of consecration is a way exempt from sacrifices and perils. One who moves in this direction is certain to encounter the adversary at every step. The moment the believer makes any determined advance toward holiness, that moment the evil one moves up his picket line for desperate resistance. Pastor Blumhardt (1805-1880), who in this generation has wrought such conquests in prayer and faith lays special emphasis on this point, telling us that "he who is ignorant of the wiles and artifices of the enemy, only beats the air, and the devil is not afraid of him."

Let the reader study the life of this remarkable man, if he would learn what possibilities of spiritual power are still open to us. Amid the freezing rationalism of Tubingen University, here was one young heart which kept itself kindled with the fire of Pentecost, and by surrendering itself up to daily consecration, was preparing to give the world a living demonstration of the things which the learned men of that university had set themselves to deny. We see him raising the sick by his prayers, casting out devils, and bringing whole communities to the foot of the cross in penitence. But Satan was always at his right hand to resist him. "In interesting myself in behalf of one possessed," he writes, "I became involved in such a fearful conflict with the powers of darkness, as is not possible for me to describe." Underscore this passage, O reader. It has a broad significance. When something extraordinary is to be done for Christ, hell from beneath will be moved to resist it. The marks of Martin Luther's (1483-1546) inkstand on Wartburg castle are not the traces of a pitiable superstition. Here is a man who is to shake all Europe with a new revival, and where on earth or under the earth is Satan so likely to mass his forces as in this monk's cell! Brother Martin is not throwing his ink horn at a phantom when he hurls it at the devil. It is very necessary to touch on this point, because every aspirant after holiness is certain to be assailed with peculiar conflicts and temptations; and it is natural to regard these as indications that dangerous ground has been entered upon, when they are often only evidences that we are entering upon higher ground.

That gifted woman in whom inspiration and aspiration were so beautifully blended, Frances Ridley Havergal (1836-1879), makes a cheering comment on a familiar text of Scripture: "Behold, I give unto you power to tread all serpents and scorpions, and over all the power of the enemy" (Luke 10:19). "Why this is grand," she writes, "Power over all the power of the enemy. Just where he is strongest, there they shall prevail. Not over his weak points and places, but over the very centre of his power; not over his power here and there, or now and then, but over all his power. And Jesus said it. Isn't it enough to go into battle with?"[5]

She was encouraging her own heart when she wrote these words. What a lofty path of spirituality she traversed! Has the reader of her biography marked the open secret of her consecrated career? It is found in the same experience, of which we have spoken elsewhere, of definite, whole-souled devotion to God. This is the record of it, which she has left behind :

"It was on Advent Sunday, December, 1873, that I first saw clearly the blessedness of true consecration. I saw it as a flash of electric light; and what you see, you can never unsee. *There must be full surrender before there can be full blessedness, God admits you by the one into the other.* He Himself showed me this most clearly. You know how singularly I have been withheld from attending conventions and conferences; man's teaching has consequently but little to do with it. First I was shown that the blood of Jesus Christ, His Son, cleanseth from all sin; and then it was made plain to me that He who had thus cleansed me, had power to keep me clean; so I utterly yielded myself to Him and utterly trusted Him to keep me."

In literature and in life, she served her generation with rare effectiveness. Her works are suffused with a beautiful glow of spiritual health; and in reading her books of sacred poetry and devotion, honored with an almost unprecedented circulation, we wonder if anyone in our clay has spoken more directly to the heart of man, and more directly from the heart of God. And thus the lesson is pressed upon us anew of the power of a sanctified life.

In treating thus of special acts of consecration, we would interpose a caution against written covenants with God. To yield ourselves up to him in full self-surrender is one thing; to bind ourselves to do and to suffer certain things for him is quite another. The Divine nature within us may be strong enough to perform such vows, but human nature is insolvent, and all its promises are but a bankrupt's bond. And this human nature is still a partner in the firm that makes the contract, just as our Lord so solemnly declared in the face of his disciples' failure and desertion. "The spirit indeed is willing, but the flesh weak" (Matt. 26:41).

Dr. Philip Doddridge (1702-1751) recommended a written compact with the Lord. "Set your hand and seal to it, that on such a day of such a month and year, and at such a place, on full consideration and serious reflection, you came to the happy resolution, that whatever others might do, you would serve the Lord." The excellent Samuel Pearce of Birmingham (1766-1799) followed this advice in his early Christian life. He wrote his solemn league and covenant with God, and to make it the more binding he opened a vein in his arm and signed it with his own blood. But when in a little while he found how utterly he had broken this sacred engagement, he was plunged into despair, and only found release when he tore up the document and scattered it to the winds, and cast himself henceforth entirely upon the "blood of the everlasting covenant" (Heb. 13:20)"[6]

We do not say that such a method can never be of use. It may in some instances. John Frederick Oberlin (1740-1826), the devoted and apostolic pastor, seems to have found it so. He certainly furnishes another striking illustration of the influence of definite and entire consecration. Let one read of the astonishing change effected through his ministry in the morals and condition of his little flock in Waldbach, amid the wilds of Northern France. Or let one ponder the exquisite story of the orphan girl, Louise Schepler (1763-1837), so impressed by the holiness and self-denial of this good pastor's life, that she begged the privilege of serving him without wages or reward, so long as she should live. The clue to his remarkable power may doubtless be found in a document which was left among his papers. It is long, but we give a paragraph which contains its pith and substance.

"In the name of the Lord of hosts, I this day renounce all former lords that have had dominion over me, the joys of the world in which I have too much delighted, and all carnal desires. I renounce all perishable things in order that God may constitute my All. I consecrate to Thee all that I am, and all that I have; the faculties of my mind, the members of my body, my fortune, and my time. Grant me grace, O Father of mercies, to employ all to Thy glory, and in obedience to Thy commands. For ardently and humbly I desire to be Thine through the endless ages of eternity. Should Thou be pleased to make me in this life the instrument in leading others to Thee, give me strength and courage openly to declare Thy Name. And enable me, not only to devote myself to Thy service, but to persuade my brethren to dedicate themselves to it also." Signed: *Strasbourg, 1st January, 1760. Renewed at Waldbach, 1st January, 1770.*[7]

We have given quite enough in these examples to exhibit the intimate and certain relation of personal consecration to spiritual power. But in all that we have said, we have assumed that the Holy Spirit is the Sanctifier and Sealer of this consecration. Our Lord Jesus Christ here, as in all things, is our Pattern and Exemplar. "For their sakes I sanctify myself, that they also might be sanctified through the truth" (John 17:19). Exemplar, we said. He is more than this—He is our life. It is his Divine nature working in us which can alone effect this great transaction. He acted in and through the Holy Spirit in his self-devotion—"who through the eternal Spirit offered himself without spot to God" (Heb. 9:14). How much more must we rely upon that Divine inworking! We need the Spirit by whom to seek the Spirit, Christ's consecration by which to consecrate ourselves, God's supreme gift, the Comforter, by whom to give ourselves to God.

O, Holy Spirit, who dost make our bodies Thy habitation, consecrate that in which Thou dost dwell, that it may be "a vessel unto honor, sanctified and meet for the Master's use, and prepared unto every good work" (2 Tim. 2:21).

Source for Chapter 14: A. J. Gordon, *The Twofold Life* (London: Hodder and Stoughton, 1900), 31-48. Retrieved from: http://www. gordon.edu/page.cfm?iPageID=1805.

CHAPTER 15

The Enduement of the Spirit

To the disciples, the baptism of the Spirit was very distinctly not his first bestowal for regeneration, but the definite communication of his presence in power of their glorified Lord. Just as there was a twofold operation of the one Spirit in the Old and New Testaments, of which the state of the disciples before and after Pentecost was the striking illustration, so there may be, and in the great majority of Christians is, a corresponding difference of experience . . . when once the distinct recognition of what the indwelling of the Spirit was meant to bring is brought home to the soul, and it is ready to give up all to be made partaker of it, the believer may ask and expect what may be termed a baptism of the Spirit. Praying to the Father in accordance to the two prayers in Ephesians, and coming to Jesus in the renewed surrender of faith and obedience, he may receive such an inflow of the Holy Spirit as shall consciously lift him to a different level from the one on which he has hitherto lived."

— Andrew Murray (1828-1917)

We have maintained that the baptism in the Holy Spirit was given once for all on the day of Pentecost, when the Paraclete came in person to make his abode in the church. It does not follow therefore that every believer has received this baptism. God's gift is one thing; our appropriation of that gift is quite another thing. Our relation to the second and to the third persons of the Godhead is exactly parallel in this respect. "God so loved the world that he *gave* his only begotten Son" (John 3:16). "But as many as *received him* to them gave he the right to become the children of God, even to them that believe on his name" (John 1:12). Here are the two sides of salvation, the Divine and the human, which are absolutely co-essential.

There is a doctrine somewhat in vogue, not inappropriately denominated redemption by incarnation, which maintains that since God gave his Son to the world, all the world has the Son, consciously or unconsciously, and that therefore all the world will be saved. It need not be said that a true evangelical teaching must reject this theory as utterly untenable, since it ignores the necessity of individual faith in Christ. But some orthodox writers have urged an almost identical view with respect to the Holy Spirit. They have contended that the enduement of the Spirit is "not any special or more advanced experience, but simply the condition of everyone who is a child of God"; that "believers converted after Pentecost, and living in other localities, are just as really endowed with the indwelling Spirit as those who actually partook of the Pentecostal blessing at Jerusalem."[1]

On the contrary, it seems clear from the Scriptures that it is still the duty and privilege of believers to receive the Holy Spirit by a conscious, definite act of appropriating faith, just as they received Jesus Christ. We base this conclusion on several grounds. Presumably if the Paraclete is a person, coming down at a certain definite time to make his abode in the church, for guiding, teaching, and sanctifying the body of Christ, there is the same reason for our accepting him for his special ministry as for accepting the Lord Jesus for his special ministry. To say that in receiving Christ we necessarily received in the same act the gift of the Spirit, seems to confound what the Scriptures make distinct.[2] For it is as sinners that we accept Christ for our justification, but it is as sons that we accept the Spirit for our sanctification: "And because ye are sons, God hath sent forth the Spirit of his Son into your hearts, crying Abba, Father" (Gal. 4:6). Thus, when Peter preached his first sermon to the multitude after the Spirit had been given, he said: "Repent and be baptized, everyone of you, in the name of Jesus Christ, for the remission of sins, and ye shall receive the gift of the Holy Spirit" (Acts 2:38).

This passage shows that logically and chronologically the gift of the Spirit is subsequent to repentance. Whether it follows as a necessary and inseparable consequence, as might seem, we shall consider later. Suffice that this point is clear, so clear that one of the most conservative as well as ablest writers on this subject, in commenting on this text in Acts, says:

> Therefore it is evident that the reception of the Holy Ghost, as
> here spoken of, has nothing whatever to do with bringing
> men to believe and repent. It is a subsequent operation; it is
> an additional and separate blessing; it is a privilege founded
> on faith already actively working in the heart. . . . I do not
> mean to deny that the gift of the Holy Ghost may be practi-
> cally on the same occasion, but never in the same moment.
> The reason is quite simple too. The gift of the Holy Ghost is
> grounded on the fact that we are sons by faith in Christ, be-
> lievers resting on redemption in him. Plainly, therefore, it
> appears that the Spirit of God has already regenerated us.[2]

Now, as we examine the Scriptures on this point, we shall see
that we are required to appropriate the Spirit as sons, in the same
way that we appropriated Christ as sinners. "As many as received
him, even to them that believe on his name" (John 1:12), is the condition of becoming sons, as we have already seen, receiving and believing being used as equivalent terms. In a kind of foretaste of Pentecost,
the risen Christ, standing in the midst of his disciples, "breathed on
them and said, 'Receive ye the Holy Spirit'" (John 20:22). The verb is
not passive, as our English version might lead us to suppose, but has
here as generally an active signification, just as in the familiar passage
in Revelation: "Whosoever will, let him *take* the water of life
freely" (Rev. 21:6). Twice in the Epistle to the Galatians the possession
of the Holy Spirit is put on the same grounds of active appropriation
through faith: "Received ye the Spirit by the works of the law or by
the hearing of faith?" (3 : 2). "That ye might receive the promise of the
Spirit through faith" (3:14). These texts seem to imply that just as
there is a "faith toward our Lord Jesus Christ" (Acts 20:21) for salvation, there is a faith toward the Holy Spirit for power and consecration.

If we turn from New Testament teaching to New Testament example we are strongly confirmed in this impression. We begin with
that striking incident in the nineteenth chapter of Acts. Paul, having
found certain disciples at Ephesus, said unto them: "Did ye receive

the Holy Spirit when ye believed? And they said unto him, Nay; we did not so much as hear whether there is a Holy Spirit" (Acts 19:2). This passage seems decisive as showing that one may be a disciple without having entered into possession of the Spirit as God's gift to believers. Some admit this, who yet deny any possible application of the incident to our own times, alleging that it is the miraculous gifts of the Spirit which are here under consideration, since, after recording that when Paul had laid his hands upon them and "the Holy Spirit came upon them," it is added that "they spake with tongues and prophesied" (Acts 19:6). All that need be said upon this point is simply that these Ephesian disciples, by the reception of the Spirit, came into the same condition with the upper room disciples who received him some twenty years before, and of whom it is written that "they were all filled with the Holy Spirit and began to speak with other tongues as the Spirit gave them utterance" (Acts 2:2). In other words, these Ephesian disciples on receiving the Holy Spirit exhibited the traits of the Spirit common to the other disciples of the apostolic age.

Whether those traits—the speaking of tongues and the working of miracles—were intended to be perpetual or not we do not here discuss. But that the presence of the personal Holy Spirit in the church was intended to be perpetual there can be no question. And whatever relations believers held to that Spirit in the beginning they have a right to claim today. We must withhold our consent from the inconsistent exegesis which would make the water baptism of the apostolic times still rigidly binding, but would relegate the baptism in the Spirit to a bygone dispensation. We hold indeed, that Pentecost was once for all, but equally that the appropriation of the Spirit by believers is always for all, and that the shutting up of certain great blessings of the Holy Spirit within that ideal realm called "the apostolic age," however convenient it may be as an escape from fancied difficulties, may be the means of robbing believers of some of their most precious covenant rights.[4]

Let us transfer this incident of the Ephesian Christians to our own times. We need not bring forward an imaginary case, for by the testimony of many experienced witnesses the same condition is constantly encountered. Not only individual Christians, but whole communities of disciples are found who have been so imperfectly instructed that they have never known that there is a Holy Spirit, except as an influence, an impersonal something to be vaguely recognized. Of the Holy Spirit as a Divine Person, dwelling in the church, to be honored and invoked and obeyed and implicitly trusted, they know nothing. Is it conceivable that there could be any deep spiritual life or any real sanctified energy for service in a community like this? And what should a well-instructed teacher or evangelist do, on discovering a church or an individual Christian in such a condition? Let us turn to another passage of the Acts for an answer: "Now when the apostles which were at Jerusalem heard that Samaria had received the word of God they sent unto them Peter and John, who when they were come down prayed for them that they might receive the Holy Spirit; for as yet he had fallen upon none of them; only they were baptized in the name of the Lord Jesus. Then laid they their hands on them and they received the Holy Spirit" (Acts 8:14-17).

Here were believers who had been baptized in water. But this was not enough. The baptism in the Spirit, already bestowed at Pentecost, must be appropriated. Hear the prayer of the apostles "that they might receive the Holy Spirit." Such prayer we deem eminently proper for those who today may be ignorant of the Comforter. And yet such prayer should be followed by an act of believing acceptance on the part of the willing disciple: *"O Holy Spirit, I yield to thee now in humble surrender. I receive thee as my Teacher, my Comforter, my Sanctifier, and my Guide."* Do not testimonies abound on every hand of new lives resulting from such an act of consecration as this, lives full of peace and power and victory among those who before had received the forgiveness of sins but not the enduement of power?

We conceive that the great end for which the enduement of the Spirit is bestowed is our qualification for the highest and most effective service in the church of Christ. Other effects will certainly attend the blessing, a fixed assurance of our acceptance in Christ, and a holy separation from the world; but these results will be conducive to the greatest and supreme end, our consecrated usefulness.

Let us observe that Christ, who is our example in this as in all things, did not enter upon his ministry till he had received the Holy Spirit. Not only so, but we see that all his service from his baptism to his ascension was wrought in the Spirit. Ask concerning his miracles,

119

and we hear him saying: "I by the Spirit of God cast out devils" (Matt. 12: 28). Ask concerning that death which he accomplished at Jerusalem, and we read "that he through the eternal Spirit offered himself without spot unto God" (Heb. 9:14). Ask concerning the giving of the great commission, and we read that he was received up "after that he through the Holy Spirit had given commandments unto the apostles" (Acts 1:2). Thus, though he was the Son of God, he acted ever in supreme reliance upon him who has been called the "Executive of the Godhead."

Plainly we see how Christ was our pattern and exemplar in his relation to the Holy Spirit. He had been begotten of the Holy Spirit in the womb of the virgin, and had lived that holy and obedient life which this Divine nativity would imply. But when he would enter upon his public ministry, he waited for the Spirit to come upon him, as he had hitherto been in him. For this anointing we find him praying: "Jesus also being baptized and praying, the heaven was opened, and the Holy Spirit descended in a bodily shape like a dove upon him" (Luke 3:22). Had he any promise of the Father to plead, as he now asked for the anointing of the Spirit, if as we may believe this was the subject of his prayer?

Yes, it had been written in the prophets concerning the rod out of the stem of Jesse: "And the Spirit of the Lord shall rest upon him; the Spirit of wisdom and understanding, the Spirit of counsel and might, the Spirit of knowledge and of the fear of the Lord" (Isa. 11:2). "The promise of the sevenfold Spirit," the Jewish commentators call it. Certainly it was literally fulfilled upon the Son of God at the Jordan, when God gave him the Spirit without measure. For he who was now baptized was in turn to be baptizer. "Upon whom thou shalt see the Spirit descending, and remaining on him, the same is he which baptizeth with the Holy Spirit" (John 1:33). "I indeed baptize you in water unto repentance: but he that cometh after me is mightier than I, . . . he shall baptize you in the Holy Spirit and in fire" (Matt. 3:11). And now being at the right hand exalted, and having "the seven spirits of God" (Rev. 3:3), the fullness of the Holy Spirit, Christ will shed forth his power upon those who pray for it, even as the Father shed it forth upon himself.

Source for Chapter 15: A. J. Gordon, *The Ministry of the Spirit* (Philadelphia: American Baptist Publication Society, 1896), 66-76.

CHAPTER 16

Sanctification in Christ

"... to them that are sanctified in Christ Jesus."
—1 Corinthians 1:2

*"But of him are ye in Christ Jesus, who of God
is made unto us ... sanctification."*
—1 Corinthians 1:30

"He that abideth in me, and I in him, the same bringeth forth much fruit."
—John 15:5

The believer's sanctification is at once both complete and incomplete. As "sanctified in Christ Jesus," and embraced in his comprehending holiness, he can no more improve this grace than he can add luster to a sunbeam. It is a work of God, and whatever God does, it shall be forever; nothing can be added to it, nor anything taken from it. As fulfilling in himself that sanctification which has been wrought for him in Jesus Christ, this grace is only too painfully partial and incomplete. For imperfection is as characteristic of the creature as perfection is of the Creator.

We shall be less likely therefore to fall into error and confusion concerning this doctrine if we keep in mind the distinction between what we are as "his workmanship" (Eph. 2:10) and what we are as "workers together with him" (2 Cor. 6:1). As the first we are not only "created in Christ Jesus" (Eph. 2:10), but "created in "righteousness and true holiness" (Eph. 4:24). Christ and his attributes never part company, and it is impossible to be made in him without being made into all that belongs to him. In the same transfiguration of faith by which we put on the Lord Jesus, do we put on his garment of holiness, "exceeding white as snow, so as no fuller on earth can white it" (Mark 9:3).

This may seem to some indeed like an assumption perilous to our humility. But do we honor God most, let it be asked, by limiting his grace to the degree of our worthiness and capacity? Is Christ best pleased that we take him piecemeal, and according to the narrow measure of what we deserve, when he has given himself to us wholly and without reference to what we deserve? No, we have no more right to find a partial sanctification in Christ than we have to find a partial justification. Both are contained in the same legacy of love, and bequeathed to us on the same condition, simple faith. "Of him are ye in Christ Jesus, who of God is made unto us wisdom and righteousness and sanctification and redemption" (1 Cor. 1:30). He is made unto us all these in their fullness, and not some of them and partially as we can receive them—unless indeed we make a distinction, which would seem unnatural, between the manner of bestowing righteousness and sanctification, holding that the one is immediately imputed and the other only gradually imparted. Would not the truth seem to be rather, that both are imputed to faith to be wrought out by obedience and holy living—God's justifying of us in Christ being more and more realized in the answer of a good conscience in ourselves, and his sanctifying or setting apart of us in Jesus being more and more fulfilled in our own sanctification or separation from sin?

And it is because we can thus rest on a completed work in Christ that we have hope to go on to completeness in ourselves, "to apprehend that for which we are apprehended of Christ Jesus" (Phil. 3:12). Hence also the harmony between texts that have seemed strangely at variance, such as, "Ye are washed and ye are sanctified" (1 Cor. 6:11), against, "This is the will of God, even your sanctification" (1 Thess. 4:3), and, "For by one offering he hath perfected forever them that are sanctified" (Heb. 10:14), against, "Let us go on unto perfection" (Heb. 6:1).

In Christ Jesus all contradictions are reconciled; the things that are incomplete, and the things that are not, becoming the things that are, and the things that are complete. As a gift of grace, then, sanctification is conferred on each Christian as soon as he believes. But it is a gift yet *held on deposit*, if we may say so, "hid with Christ in God" (Col. 3:3), to be appropriated through daily communion and gradual apprehension. And so, while the believer's realized sanctification appears painfully meager—at most a thin line of light, like the crescent of the new moon—he yet sees it ever complemented by the clear outlines of that rounded perfection which is his in the Lord Jesus, and into which he is to be daily waxing till he attains to "the measure of the stature of the fullness of Christ" (Eph. 4:13).

Is not the most fruitful root of misconception on this subject to be found in the idea, that while our justification stands wholly in Christ, our sanctification stands in ourselves? As though it were our human nature that is to be improved and brought to ultimate perfection! One surely could never harbor such an error, were he mindful of that form of doctrine to which he was committed in baptism, that declared the putting off and burial of the old man, and the putting on of the new man. And it cannot be that this forecast of the Christian life is so reversed that we are now called to exhume what has been buried, and to clothe ourselves again in the cast-off garments which we have solemnly declared to be beyond the hope of renovation. No! what has been crucified must be mortified, what has been buried must be kept down. So hopeless and irreparable is the doom of the flesh, that we know not that it is any better in the believer than in the unbeliever, only that its instincts are repressed, and its dominion circumscribed. "In me, that is, in my flesh, dwelleth no good thing" (Rom. 7:18).

Whither, then, shall I turn in my deep desire to attain a sinless life, a fruitful obedience, and a holy walk? Even unto him who, having begotten holy desires within me, is able "to give unto them their meat in due season" (Matt. 24:45), and who, having clothed me with salvation as with a garment, can also nourish and build me up in inward sanctity and perfection. Let us note then how, as every condition of our accredited sanctification rests on our being in Christ, so every condition of our practical sanctification rests on our abiding or continuing in Christ.

In the first place, sanctification implies holiness. To the question, How shall I attain a sinless life? The Word has but one answer: "in him is no sin; whosoever abideth in him sinneth not" (1 John 3:6). As the soul that is in him through the union of faith, is covered with his stainless righteousness, so that soul abiding in him in the unbroken fellowship of love and obedience, is filled with his sinless life. It sins not actively, since its activities are for the time controlled by him, and so the principle of evil is inoperative and lying in abeyance. Not that the root of sin has been eradicated. This is entwined with every fiber of the carnal nature, "like ivy in an ancient wall," as John Flavel (1627 -1691) says, "which, however plucked and uprooted, can never be wholly gotten out of it till the wall is taken down." But it is kept for the time in blessed unfruitfulness, its leaf withered by the brightness of the Savior's presence.

Doubtless many Christians have known such experiences — periods of happy exemption from willful transgression, because the will has been given up to the guidance of the Holy One, seasons of communion with Christ in which the fetters of fleshly bondage have been for the while so thoroughly broken, and its cords cast away, that the favored one has almost questioned whether he was in the body or out of the body. We may note such privileged days as those which Flavel describes, when he was permitted to have such intimacy with Christ, "such ravishing tastes of heavenly joys, and such full assurance of his interest therein, that he utterly lost sight and sense of this world and all the concerns thereof." David Brainerd records those favored engagements with the Lord Jesus, when he felt within himself such "lively actings of a holy temper and heavenly disposition, such vigorous exercise of that Divine love which casts out fear," that it was literally Christ for him to live. Jonathan Edwards enjoyed that deep entering into the Divine life, which he describes as "a calm, sweet abstraction of soul from all the concerns of this world; and sometimes a kind of vision or fixed idea of being alone in the mountains, or some solitary wilderness far from all mankind, sweetly conversing with Christ, and rapt and swallowed up in God."

But surely never more than after such abundant manifestations of the power of the Divine grace to lift one beyond the control of the flesh and into uninterrupted communion with Christ, does he need to be warned to take heed, lest, thinking that he thereby stands in a state of sinless perfection, he suddenly falls. There is a wide difference between a present attainment and a permanent attainment. And who has not found that it is easier to rise to lofty heights than it is to maintain one's self there? These grapes of Eschol, these "days of heaven," full of deep communion and freedom from conscious sin, remind us, by their very rarity and infrequency, that we have not yet reached the promised land of perfect holiness. But they tell us where to find that land—not back, beyond the waters of our baptism, in the Egypt of the flesh and in the bondage of the law—but onward over that Jordan of death in which we shall put off this corruptible forever; in that land which the Lord has given to us for an inheritance, where we shall abide continually in Christ, because separated forever from the root of Adam.

Such wild dreams as that of perfection in the flesh would be little entertained if men kept clearly in view the distinction between what we are *in Christ* and what we are *in ourselves*. To be in him is to be saved at once and forever from the condemnation of sin, but as the lives of the highest and the lowest saints alike testify, not immediately from the presence and inworking of sin. Christ had sin upon him, though he had no sin in him. He that is in Christ has no sin upon him, though he still has sin in him. And just in proportion to the completeness of his abiding in him by communion and obedience, will he be free from sin within him as he is from sin upon him.

But let us not be deceived. Because the Spirit addresses us as those that are "sanctified in the name of the Lord Jesus" (1 Cor. 6:11), let us not therefore claim to have reached a state of practical and realized sanctification in ourselves. We are "in him," that is true, and "In him is no sin" (1 John 3:5). But "if we say that we have no sin, we deceive ourselves, and the truth is not in us" (1 John 1:8). Not yet have we reached that Paradise of holy perfection for which we sigh, that sweet millennium of inward peace and righteousness where sin can hurt and destroy no longer. For that we wait till the old leaven of the flesh has been purged out and we have become a new lump. And then when Christ who is our life shall appear—appear "without sin unto salvation" (Heb. 9:28)—shall we appear also with him in glory, without sin either in us or upon us forever.

Is death then the great sanctifier? it is impatiently asked. Is his cold hand endowed with a skill and cunning to do the work for us in a moment which the Spirit and the Word and the ordinances have failed to perfect in a lifetime? No, death is but the letting go of a hand that has been constantly hindering that work, the final relinquishment of his hold on the part of that carnal man who is neither subject to the law of God himself, nor permits the believer in whom he dwells to be subject to it.[1] This much negatively, and then it is also the rending of the veil that keeps us from full communion with the Lord. For to be with Christ where he is, whether that presence be gained by our going to him or by his coming to us, is doubtless essential to a state of complete abiding in him, and hence of full conformity to him.

Who knows what depth of meaning is hidden in that, "For we shall see him as he is" (1 John 3:2), in which, John finds the reason and pledge of our likeness to Christ at his appearing? All our holiness is in him and from him, as the sunbeams are in and of the sun. But how is its luster dimmed in passing through the medium of our fleshly life, and how are its rays broken and refracted before they fall upon the retina of our inward eye. Only in the open vision of his face and in his light who is the Light, can our likeness to him be rendered perfect. For only thus can we truly reflect his purity, seeing him as he is, and having the last germs of impurity in ourselves consumed in that light which is above the brightness of the sun. It is not only that our Lord will give us more of himself, but will give it, in the words of Adelaide Newton (1824-1854), "directly from Himself in place of its coming through an 'earthen vessel,' which both limits the abounding flow of his fullness and also gives an earthy taste to the living water."

And what we have said of holiness applies equally to another element of progressive sanctification, its very evidence and attestation indeed, Christian fruitfulness. This is from Jesus Christ only. "He that abideth in me and in him, the same bringeth forth much fruit" (John 15:5). In him by faith, and hence one with him in that unchangeable justification which enwraps the Head and the members together, we may be very far from abiding in him by that full communion through which his life flows into us without interruption, and abides in us without stint. The feeble branch may be in the trunk as truly as the fruitful one, knit into its structure by the same compactness of grain and fiber. But because it has little communion with it through the vital sap, it bears little fruit, and adorns its station with little greenness and beauty. Christ our Vine is not restricted in himself, but only in us. As impossible as it is for the fruits of holiness to grow upon the stock of human nature, so impossible is it for anything else to grow upon the Divine. That which is born of God cannot commit sin. It is only a question of presenting such an open channel for the inflow of the life of Jesus, that the holy principle shall be transmitted to us without obstruction, and reproduce itself without restraint.

Is there not a painful tendency among believers to seek fruit from without instead of from within, and to be satisfied with such good works as are the mere external adornment of faith instead of its direct outgrowth? But whether we speak of fulfilling righteousness in ourselves or toward others, the same principle obtains, that "whatsoever is not of faith," and hence not of Christ, "is sin" (Rom. 14:23). For sanctification we have not to copy another's holiness, however excellent, but to work out *our own* salvation; to unfold to its utmost limit that Divine life which is ours in Christ. And for service the law is the same. Love to neighbor and self-denial for mankind are to be no borrowed graces, lent us either by philanthropy or the law.

With the disciples, who so significantly met our Lord's demand for a sevenfold forgiveness of a sevenfold offense, with the prayer, "Increase our faith," (Luke 17:5), we shall learn more and more that the only way to augment the fruits of charity and longsuffering is to strike the roots of our faith more deeply into Christ, and entwine them more intimately about that cross from which the first fruits of Divine forgiveness were gathered, and from which all subsequent fruit must also spring. So directly indeed is likeness to Christ dependent upon communion with Christ, that John makes the two equivalent terms. "He that saith he abideth in him ought himself also so to walk even as he walked" (1 John 2:6). Relationship to him determines all other relationships, those of conformity to God and those of nonconformity to the world alike. Adjust the heart therefore to him, and the world is sure to be in its proper place. Put on Christ, and you are certain to put off sin. If you are clothed with the sun, the moon (all sublunary things) will be under your feet.

If from the conditions, we turn to consider the means of sanctification, we see how obviously these are such, because they are the media of communion with Christ, and participants in his life.

"Sanctify them *through thy truth*" (John 17:17), the truth not only as it is in Jesus, but as Jesus is in it. For the Word, it need not be said, is the earthly repository of Christ, filled by his informing presence, and vital with all the yet undiscovered meanings of his hidden wisdom. Therefore is it able to be the daily bread of the soul, and to satisfy all possible cravings of its Divine hunger. "Thy words were found of me, and I did eat them" (Jer. 15:16).

"Chosen to salvation *through sanctification of the Spirit*" (2 Thess. 2:13). The Holy One whose office it is to take of the things of Christ and show them to us. For this we must always remember, that he does not speak of himself. He brings "the Life" to our life, and makes the sanctified One to be more and more our sanctification, until we are filled with all his fullness.

Thus slowly, and as it may seem to us quite imperceptibly, is God bringing this Divine work to completion in us. Blessed are they who shrink not from the sharper but not less needed means of its accomplishment, those trials and chastisements, those humiliations and self-denials, which are the pangs of transformation through which Christ is to be fully formed within us. "Though our outward man perish, yet the inward man is renewed day by day" (2 Cor. 4:16). "The more the marble wastes, the more the statue grows," wrote Michael Angelo (1475-1564).

And impossible as it will be for nature, let it not be impossible for grace to cry daily, "Welcome cross, welcome trials, welcome all things sweet or bitter, which shall bring forth within us that perfect man, that Divine ideal, visible ever to the eye of God, and growing more and more upon our sight as we grow up into him who is our Head."

Source for Chapter 16: A. J. Gordon, *In Christ* (Grand Rapids: Baker, 1964), 167-182. Reprinted from the 1872 edition by Gould and Lincoln, Boston. Retrieved from: http://www.gordon. edu/page.cfm? iPageID=1805.

CHAPTER 17

The Spirit of Holiness: Our Sanctification

But we all with unveiled face, reflecting as a mirror the glory of the Lord, are transformed into the same image from glory to glory, even as from the Lord, the Spirit.

—2 Corinthians 3:18 RV

"According to the Spirit of holiness," Christ "was declared to be the Son of God in power by the resurrection from the dead" (Rom. 1:4). How striking the antithesis between our Lord's two natures, as revealed in this passage, Son of David as to the flesh, Son of God as to the Spirit. And "as he is so are we in this world" (1 John 4:17). We who are regenerate have two natures, the one derived from Adam, the other derived from Christ, and our sanctification consists in the double process of mortification and vivification, the deadening and subduing of the old and the quickening and developing of the new. In other words, what was wrought in Christ who was "put to death in the flesh but quickened in the Spirit" (1 Pet. 3:18) is re-wrought in us through the constant operation of the Holy Spirit, and thus the cross and the resurrection extend their sway over the entire life of the Christian. Consider these two experiences.

Mortification is not asceticism. It is not a self-inflicted compunction, but a Christ-inflicted crucifixion. Our Lord was done with the cross when on Calvary he cried: "It is finished" (John 19:30). But where he ended each disciple must begin: "If any man will come after me let him deny himself and take up his cross and follow me. For whosoever will save his life shall lose it, and whosoever will lose his life for my sake shall find it" (Matt. 16:24-25). These words, so constantly repeated in one form or another by our Lord, make it clear that the death principle must be realized within us in order that the life-principle may have final and triumphant sway. It is to this truth which every disciple is solemnly committed in his baptism: "Know ye not that so many of us as were baptized into Christ were baptized into his death? Therefore we were buried with him by baptism into death, that like as Christ was raised up from the dead by the glory of the Father, even so we also should walk in newness of life" (Rom. 6:3-4). Baptism is the monogram of the Christian; by it every believer is sealed and certified as a participant in the death and life of Christ; and the Holy Spirit has been given to be the Executor of the contract thus made at the symbolic grave of Christ.

In considering the great fact of the believer's death in Christ to sin and the law, we must not confound what the Scriptures clearly distinguish. There are three deaths in which we have part: 1) death in sin, our natural condition; 2) death for sin, our judicial condition; 3) death to sin, our sanctified condition.

1. *Death in sin.* "And you . . . who were dead in trespasses and sins," "And you being dead in your sins" (Eph. 2:1; Col. 2:13). This is the condition in which we are by nature, as participants in the fall and ruin into which the transgression of our first parents has plunged the race. It is a condition in which we are under moral insensibility to the claims of God's holiness and love; and under the sentence of eternal punishment from the law which we have broken. In this state of death in sin Christ found the whole world when he came to be our Savior.

2. *Death for sin.* "Wherefore, my brethren, ye also are become dead to the law by the body of Christ" (Rom. 7:4). This is the condition into which Christ brought us by his sacrifice upon the cross. He endured the sentence of a violated law on our behalf, and therefore we are counted as having endured it in him. What he did for us is

reckoned as having been done by us: "Because we thus judge, that one died for all, therefore all died" (2 Cor. 5:14 RV). Being one with Christ through faith, we are identified with him on the cross: "I have been crucified with Christ" (Gal. 2:20 RV). This condition of death for sin having been effected for us by our Savior, we are held legally or judicially free from the penalty of a violated law, if by our personal faith we will consent to the transaction.

3. *Death to sin.* "Even so reckon ye also yourselves to be dead unto sin, but alive unto God in Christ Jesus" (Rom. 6:11 RV). This is the condition of making true in ourselves what is already true for us in Christ, of rendering practical what is now judicial. In other words, of being dead to the power of sin in ourselves, as we are already dead to the penalty of sin through Jesus Christ. As it is written in the Epistle to the Colossians: "For ye died," judicially in Christ, "mortify"—make dead practically—"therefore your members which are upon the earth" (Col. 3:2, 5 RV).

It is this condition which the Holy Spirit is constantly effecting in us if we will have it so: "If ye through the Spirit do mortify the deeds of the body ye shall live" (Rom. 8:13). This is not self-deadening, as the Revised Version seems to suggest by its de-capitalizing of the word " Spirit." Self is not powerful enough to conquer self, the human spirit to get the victory over the human flesh. That would be like a drowning man with his right hand laying hold on his left hand, only that both may sink beneath the waves. "Old Adam is too strong for young Melancthon," said the Reformer (1497-1560). It is the Spirit of God overcoming our fleshly nature by his indwelling life, on whom is our sole dependence. Our principal care therefore must be to "walk in the Spirit" and "be filled with the Spirit" (Gal. 5:16; Eph. 5:18), and all the rest will come spontaneously and inevitably. As the ascending sap in the tree crowds off the dead leaves which in spite of storm and frost cling to the branches all winter long, so does the Holy Spirit within us, when allowed full sway, subdue and expel the remnants of our sinful nature.

One cannot fail to see that asceticism is an absolute inversion of the Divine order, since it seeks life through death instead of finding death through life. No degree of mortification can ever bring us to sanctification. We are to "put off the old man with his deeds" (Col. 3:9). But how? By "putting on the new man who is renewed in knowledge after the image of him that created him" (Col. 3:10). "For the law of the Spirit of life in Christ Jesus hath made me free from the law of sin and death" (Rom. 8:2), writes Paul. It is a pointed statement of the case, which one makes in describing the transition from the old to the new in his own experience, from the former life of perpetual defeat to the present life of victory through Christ. "Once it was a constant breaking off, now it is a daily bringing in," he says. That is, the former striving was directed to being rid of the inveterate habits and evil tendencies of the old nature—its selfishness, its pride, its lust, and its vanity. Now the effort is to bring in the Spirit, to drink in his Divine presence, to breathe, as a holy atmosphere, his supernatural life. The indwelling of the Spirit can alone effect the exclusion of sin. This will appear if we consider what has been called "the expulsive power of a new affection." "Love not the world, neither the things that are in the world" (1 John 2:15), says the Scripture. But all experience proves that loving not is only possible through loving, the worldly affection being overcome by the heavenly.

And we find this method clearly exhibited in the Word. "The love of the Spirit" (Rom. 15:30) is given us for overcoming the world. The Divine life is the source of the Divine love. Therefore "the love of God is shed abroad in our hearts by the Holy Spirit which is given unto us" (Rom. 5:5). Because we are by nature so wholly without heavenly affection, God, through the indwelling Spirit, gives us his own love with which to love himself. Herein is the highest credential of discipleship: "By this shall all men know that ye are my disciples, if ye have love one to another" (John 13:35). As Christ manifested to the world the love of the Father, so are we to manifest the love of Christ—a manifestation, however, which is only possible because of our possession of a common life.

As one has truly said concerning our Savior's command to his disciples to love one another: "It is a command which would be utterly idle and futile were it not that he, the ever-loving One, is willing to put his own love within me. The command is really no more than to be a branch of the true vine. I am to cease from my own living and loving, and yield myself to the expression of Christ's love."

And what is true of the love of Christ is true of the likeness of Christ. How is the likeness acquired? Through contemplation and imitation? So some have taught. And it is true, if only the indwelling Spirit is behind all, beneath all, and effectually operative in all. As it is written: "But we all with unveiled face, reflecting as a mirror the glory of the Lord, are transformed into the same image from glory to glory, even as from the Lord, the Spirit" (2 Cor. 3:18 RV). It is only the Spirit of the Lord dwelling within us that can fashion us to the image of the Lord set before us. Who is sufficient by external imitation of Christ to become conformed to the likeness of Christ? Imagine one without genius and devoid of the artist's training sitting down before Raphael's famous picture of the Transfiguration and attempting to reproduce it. How crude and mechanical and lifeless his work would be!

But if such a thing were possible that the spirit of Raphael should enter into the man and obtain the mastery of his mind and eye and hand, it would be entirely possible that he should paint this masterpiece; for it would simply be Raphael reproducing Raphael. And this in a mystery is what is true of the disciple filled with the Holy Spirit. Christ, who is "the image of the invisible God" (Col. 1:15), is set before him as his Divine pattern, and Christ by the Spirit dwells within him as a Divine life, and Christ is able to image forth Christ from the interior life to the outward example.

Of course likeness to Christ is but another name for holiness, and when, at the resurrection, we awake satisfied with his likeness (Psa. 17:15), we shall be perfected in holiness. This is simply saying that sanctification is progressive and not, like conversion, instantaneous. And yet we must admit the force of what a devout and thoughtful writer says as to the danger of regarding it as only a gradual growth. If a Christian looks upon himself as "a tree planted by the rivers of water that bringeth forth his fruit in his season," he judges rightly. But to conclude therefore that his growth will be as irresistible as that of the tree, coming as a matter of course simply because he has by regeneration been planted in Christ, is a grave mistake. The disciple is required to be consciously and intelligently active in his own growth, as a tree is not, "to give all diligence to make his calling and election sure" (2 Pet. 1:10). And when we say "active" we do not mean self-active merely, for "which of you by being anxious can add one cubit unto his stature?" asks Jesus (Matt. 6:27 RV). But we must surrender ourselves to the Divine action by living in the Spirit and praying in the Spirit and walking in the Spirit, all of which conditions are as essential to our development in holiness, as the rain and the sunshine are to the growth of the oak. It is possible that through a neglect and grieving of the Spirit a Christian may be of smaller stature in his age than he was in his spiritual infancy, his progress being a retrogression rather than an advance. Therefore in saying that sanctification is progressive let us beware of concluding that it is inevitable.

Moreover, as candid inquirers, we must ask what of truth and of error there may be in the doctrine of "instantaneous sanctification," which many devout persons teach and profess to have proved. If the conception is that of *a state of sinless perfection* into which the believer has been suddenly lifted and of deliverance from a sinful nature which has been suddenly eradicated, we must consider this doctrine as dangerously untrue. But we do consider it possible that one may experience a great crisis in his spiritual life, in which there is such a total self-surrender to God and such an infilling of the Holy Spirit, that he is *freed from the bondage of sinful appetites and habits,* and enabled to have *constant victory* over self, instead of suffering constant defeat. In saying this, what more do we affirm than is taught in that scripture: "Walk in the Spirit and ye shall not fulfill the lust of the flesh" (Gal. 5:16).

Divine truth as revealed in Scripture seems often to lie between two extremes. It is emphatically so in regard to this question. What a paradox it is that side by side in the First Epistle of John we should have the strongest affirmation of the Christian's sinfulness: "If we say that we have no sin we deceive ourselves, and the truth is not in us"; and the strongest affirmation of his sinlessness: "Whosoever is born of God doth not commit sin, for his seed remaineth in him, and he cannot sin because he is born of God" (1 John 1:8; 3:9). Now heresy means a dividing or choosing, and almost all of the gravest errors have arisen from adopting some extreme statement of Scripture to the rejection of the other extreme. *If we regard the doctrine of sinless perfec-*

tion as a heresy, we regard contentment with sinful imperfection as a greater heresy. And we gravely fear that many Christians make the apostle's words, "If we say we have no sin we deceive ourselves," the unconscious justification for a low standard of Christian living. It were almost better for one to overstate the possibilities of sanctification in his eager grasp after holiness, than to understate them in his complacent satisfaction with a traditional un-holiness. Certainly it is not an edifying spectacle to see a Christian worldling throwing stones at a Christian perfectionist.

What then would be a true statement of the doctrine which we are considering, one which would embrace both extremes of statement as they appear in the First Epistle of John? *Sinful in self, sinless in Christ* — is our answer: "In him is no sin; whosoever abideth in him sinneth not" (1 John 3:5-6). If through the communication of the Holy Spirit the life of Christ is constantly imparted to us, that life will prevail within us. That life is absolutely sinless, as incapable of defilement as the sunbeam which has its fount and origin in the sun. In proportion to the closeness of our abiding in him will be the completeness of our deliverance from sinning. And we doubt not that there are Christians who have yielded themselves to God in such absolute surrender, and who through the upholding power of the Spirit have been so kept in that condition of surrender, that sin has not had dominion over them. If in them the war between the flesh and the Spirit has not been forever ended, there has been present victory in which troublesome sins have ceased from their assaults, and "the peace of God" has ruled in the heart.

But sinning is one thing and a sinful nature is another; and we see no evidence in Scripture that the latter is ever eradicated completely while we are in the body. If we could see ourselves with God's eye, we should doubtless discover sinfulness lying beneath our most joyful moments of un-sinning conduct, and the stain of our old and fallen nature so discoloring our whitest actions as to convince us that we are not yet faultless in his presence. Only let us gladly emphasize this fact, that as we inherit from Adam a nature incapable of sinlessness, we inherit from Christ a nature incapable of sinfulness. Therefore, it is written: "Whosoever is born of God cannot sin, for his seed remaineth in him" (1 John 3:9). It is not the nature of the new nature to sin; it is not the law of "the law of the Spirit of life" (Rom. 8:2) to transgress, For the new-born man to do evil is to transgress the law of his nature as before it was to obey it. In a word, before our regeneration we lived in sin and loved it; since our regeneration we may lapse into sin but we loathe it.

Source for Chapter 17: A. J. Gordon, *The Ministry of the Spirit* (Philadelphia: American Baptist Publication Society, 1896), 107-118.

CHAPTER 18

Prayer in Christ

"If ye abide in me, and my words abide in you,
ye shall ask what ye will, and it shall be done unto you."
—John 15:7

"Verily, verily I say to you, Whatsoever ye shall
ask in my name, he will give it you."
—John 16:23

Among the richest privileges growing out of Divine union is that of prayer in the name of Jesus. Indeed, it is at once the most precious fruit of the believer's life in Christ and the most powerful sustenance of that life—that by which it both holds and is held.

And yet it may be questioned whether to the mass of Christians the deepest thought of that thrice repeated promise of our Lord, "Verily, verily, I say unto you, Whatsoever ye shall ask the Father in my name he will give it you" (John 16:23), is not a hidden thought namely—that asking in the name of Christ is asking in union with the person of Christ."[1]

One common apprehension of the matter is certainly true, that the Christian is permitted to use the credit of that "name which is above every name" (Phil. 2:9) in making his request to God. And this is indeed an inestimable privilege. For we know even in human relations how much of one's personal qualities and attributes his name carries with it, how that he who is permitted to use his patron's name is thereby to a certain extent invested with that patron's character, so that whatever commercial or moral value belongs to it is for the time made over to him and becomes a personal possession. But another quite as common view of the matter is certainly not true, that any request, whatever its nature, needs only to have the words "for Christ's sake" attached to it to ensure an answer. No! To pray in Christ's name is not to use his name as a charm or talisman simply, as though the bare repetition of it were all that is required to open the treasures of infinite grace. Let us not degrade this dearest promise of our Lord into such a superstition as that. The Jewish cabalists believed that the pronunciation of certain magical words engraved on the seal of Solomon would perform miracles. That was incantation. And we in like manner make Christian incantation of this most sublime privilege of the gospel if we put such an interpretation as this upon Christ's words.

The name of Christ stands for Christ himself. And to pray in the name of Christ is to pray in Christ, in the mind and spirit and will of Christ. "If ye abide in me, and my words abide in you, ye shall ask what ye will, and it shall be done unto you" (John 15:7).

To repeat a holy name is an easy thing; but to attain that holy abiding in which there is such a perfect community of life with our true Vine, that it is as impossible for us to ask amiss as for the branch of the fig tree to put forth the buds and flowers of the thorn, is, as we all confess, to reach the very highest ideal of discipleship. And yet on nothing short of this perfection of union with our Lord has he predicated an unrestricted access to the treasuries of Divine blessing. The same condition is affixed to each of the highest and most longed-for attainments of the Christian life — sinlessness (1 John 3:6), fruitfulness (John 15:5), and prevalence in prayer: namely, "If ye abide in me."

Our desires, like the bud upon the tree, are the most concrete and perfect expression of ourselves. Just to the degree in which we are living in the flesh shall we be generating "the desires of the flesh and of the mind" (Eph. 2:3), bringing them to God in our prayers, and fulfilling them in our lives. Just to the degree in which we realize that blessed state, "I live, yet not I, but Christ liveth in me" (Gal. 2:20), will the desires of the Spirit be forming within us, unfolding in prayers that are "unto God a sweet savor of Christ" (Eph. 5:2), and maturing into the fruits of righteousness and true holiness. No mere selfish and earth-born desire can be endued with power, simply by being christened with that holy name. Nor can any longing toward God which has been truly begotten by the Spirit fail because the formula, "for Christ's sake," may be missing in its prayer. The secret of the Lord lies deeper than this—even in that full intimate fellowship with Jesus wherein our wills are perfectly in accord with his will as touching the thing we ask, and our desires an impulse of his holy mind.[2] The circuit of grace is complete and unobstructed between the Father, the Son, and the Spirit. If we wholly abide in Christ we get into its open and ever free currents, where all things are possible to us who believe, because all things are possible with God, with whom we are thus brought into full accord.

Has not a widespread skepticism grown up among Christians concerning the literalness of this great promise, "Whatsoever ye shall ask"—a limiting of God's faithfulness in giving, through an ignoring of that constant limitation to our receiving, namely, our lack of unbroken communion with Christ?

It is indeed a promise wonderful in its breadth: "If ye shall ask anything in my name, I will do it" (John 14:14). But because none may have ever fully measured it in human experience, shall it therefore be narrowed or conditioned as a Divine possibility? "Prayer," it has been said, "is so mighty an instrument that no one ever yet mastered all its keys. They sweep along the infinite scale of man's needs and God's goodness." And yet to be the perfect servant of Christ's will is to be the perfect master of prayer. To the touch of that will all its majestic octaves respond. " I knew that thou hearest me always." (John 11:42). And if we attune our wills perfectly to this Divine will, how shall not the Father with him freely give us all things!

The answer to prayer then is not contingent on the greatness or the smallness of the requests it contains, but upon the impulse which prompts them. If that impulse proceeds from our own will, the prayer is not in the name of Christ, though it relates to his kingdom. For even so great a request as the glory of God may be made from a selfish motive. But when the incentive to prayer is derived from an inward Divine operation, it is truly in the name of the Lord, and must have its answer. For it is then the effectual *inwrought* prayer that avails much.

Does this view suggest the question, What need then of prayer, since its limits are so circumscribed that to be genuine it must only be the expression of what God works in us to will and to desire? A question which may be answered by two others. First, Does the devout mind desire any larger range for its petitions than the circle of the perfectly wise and perfectly beneficent will of God? To know that our Lord had put into our hands a key which was entirely within the control of our blind, imperfect, erring wills, would be to know our constant peril of opening for ourselves some door of certain destruction. Hence, ought it not to be a ground of the deepest comfort and security to the suppliant praying in the Spirit of adoption, that he has a Father who not only will not give him a stone when he asks for bread, but will not give him a stone when he asks for a stone (see Luke 11:10 -12)? And, secondly, need it follow that the complete subjection of our will to Christ's is also a surrender of our freedom of petition? "Ask, and ye shall receive," is no less a command than that other, "Submit yourselves therefore to God" (James 4:7).

Prayer is the working of a will that is free, within a will that is sovereign. That the less must be obedient to the greater in making its requests, no more argues a yielding up its freedom, than that the greater will be moved by the less to answer those requests argues a yielding up of its sovereignty. Not only is there no infringement on the believer's spiritual liberty in the requirement that he ask in holy subjection to the will of his Lord, but on the contrary there is, as one has said, no other such witness to that liberty "as is wrapped up in prayer, man's permitted though submitted wish and will and choice,"[3] respecting all that pertains to his destiny.

But let us not forget that the necessity of a submitted will in prayer rests on something deeper than itself, even on the great sacrifice which is the groundwork of all devotion. As in justifying faith the soul is brought into union with Christ crucified and risen, so in intercessory faith it abides in this union. And because our great High Priest can never forget his cross and his blood, we may not. We may come with the utmost boldness to the throne of grace as being in him who "ever liveth to make intercession for us" (Heb. 7:25), but we shall come also with entire self-surrender as being in him "that liveth and was dead" (Rev. 1:18). And because we are "dead with him" (Rom. 6:8) we shall be careful to bring that only required sacrifice of the

Christian covenant, a crucified will. This is vital. "Good prayers never come weeping home," says Bishop Joseph Hall (1574-1656), which is certainly true of such prayers as have gone to heaven "by way of weeping cross." But are not many prayers put up in which there is no tender, tearful remembrance of that sacrificial woe which bought for us the right to pray in Christ—and yet prayers pleaded in his name "who in the days of his flesh offered up prayers and supplications with strong crying and tears unto him that was able to save him from death" (Heb. 5:7), each time saying the same words, "Not my will, but thine, be done" (Luke 22:42)?

Because we can nowhere else deal with God through the atonement without a submitted will, we cannot here. Saving faith is at once a surrender of self, and an appropriation of Jesus Christ. And interceding faith is like it—a hearty, aye, vehement yielding up of the will to God while laying hold of his all perfect will. Here we touch the secret of assurance. "And this is the confidence that we have in him, that, if we ask anything according to his will, he heareth us" (1 John 5:14). Outward diversions may break the reverential intimacy of our communion with him; the chill of worldliness may cool the pulse of fervent desire; but if the will yet moves needle-like to the one blessed point, the holy will of Jesus, and rests there, the deepest condition of prevailing prayer is realized.

If the conditions of prayer in Christ are thus profound and exacting, the blessing and privilege are inexpressibly glorious. To have Christ dwelling in us, his will encircling ours with its holy constraints, and his heart within us the fountain of all blessed desires, do we count this a rich prerogative of the gospel? What shall we say then of that grace whereunto we are called, of being so in Christ that his influence with the Father passes over upon us; so that "when we offer our prayers through his mediation it is he that prays, his love that intercedes, his blood that pleads, it is he who obtains all from his Father."[4]

There is something more for us now than the proxy of faith—the standing afar off with no ray of Divine approval falling upon us, and asking blessings for Jesus' sake. Lest we should think of the matter thus, our Lord declares with exquisite grace and tenderness, "I say not unto you that I will pray the Father for you, for the Father himself loveth you because ye have loved me, and have believed that I came out from God" (John 16:26-27). One with Jesus the Mediator, and endeared to the Father's heart by all that makes him dear, we come no longer to the throne as beggars asking alms, but as sons seeking an inheritance.

We cannot be ashamed now, that wait upon the Lord, for the glorified Son has said, "the glory which thou gavest me I have given them" (John 17:22). We cannot be afraid before him now, for the ever Beloved One has said, "thou hast loved them as thou hast loved me" (John 17:23). We cannot doubt that we have the petitions that we ask now, for being "in Christ Jesus who of God is made unto us righteousness" (1 Cor. 1:30). How can we fail to receive the promise, "The effectual fervent prayer of a righteous man availeth much" (James 5:16)? Perhaps in the presence of such a revelation as this, our greatest need of prayer may be to ask that we may not "stagger at the promise of God through unbelief" (Rom. 4:20). One who has looked deeply into this theme writes: "A poor sinner is permitted to approach the Father in all his troubles as though he were Christ. If one were internally awake he would not know how to bear himself for joy and amazement at the grant of such a privilege."[5]

And yet, in the unfoldings of redemption from Christ crucified to Christ glorified, this blessing and mystery only deepens more and more. The "no more conscience of sins" (Heb. 10:2) which we get while standing before the cross, is followed by the entering into the holy place with Christ after the veil of his flesh has been parted. His priesthood consummates what his blood has purchased. Into the "holiest" (Heb. 10:19), where the high priest could go only once a year, and then with the deepest awe, the humblest believer may now enter "boldly" by his oneness with his Lord. And where Aaron never sat down, there he is "made to sit in heavenly places in Christ Jesus" (Eph. 2:6). If a sense of his deep unworthiness before God often leads him to take up the cry, "Hide not thy face from thy servant," the Spirit, by convincing of the righteousness of Christ, immediately reassures him. If there is no veil between the Father and the Son in glory, how can there be any between the Father and those who are in the Son. As he is, so are they. His righteousness is their priestly vesture. He is the "Holiness unto the Lord" (Zech. 14:20) inscribed upon their foreheads. His promises are the golden bells that vibrate about their garments as they enter in unto God. Blessed are they who know their privilege in him. Thrice blessed they who faithfully use it, daily putting on the royal apparel and standing in the inner court of the King's house, assured of the outstretched scepter and the gracious promise, "What is thy petition? and it shall be granted thee; and what is thy request? it shall be performed" (Esth. 5:6).

Thus is prayer in its deepest significance a communion with the Father through communion with the Son.[6] Abiding in Christ we get the spirit of supplication—the blessing of "a mind clothed with inward prayer." His words abiding in us, both fix the direction of our petitions and bring often that answer which God has promised to suppliants "while they are yet speaking" (Isa. 65:24). Abiding in him we have his mind as our guide in intercession, so that if our desires be left unconstrained it will bend them to seek our highest blessing, as the diviner's rod, held in the unresisting hand, is bent to the cool sweet water courses that flow invisibly beneath the earth. In him, we are clothed with the righteousness which constitutes in the economy of grace not only our right of petition but our claim to be heard, so that as we appear in it before the mercy seat we may urge in triumphant humility God's oath and faithfulness: "Have respect to the Covenant."

If now our privileges are the measure of our duties, can we set any bounds to our obligation of Christian prayer? Where God's will is clearly revealed to us as, for example, concerning our personal holiness, "This is the will of God even your sanctification" (1 Thess. 4:3), the duty can be nothing less than to "pray without ceasing" (1 Thess. 5:17). And the assurance of an answer can be nothing less than to know, without questioning, that what we ask we shall receive.

In other matters, among the obscure and unrevealed decrees of Providence, if our assurance must be less specific, our supplication must not be less intense in searching for God's will, that when we have found it we may take it up and urge it with all the energy of a renewed and privileged soul. It is in constant asking that we learn how and what to ask. The soul, looking steadfastly into the Father's face, comes at last to read his thoughts after him; to catch, as by a Divine intuition, the indications of his will. "I will guide thee with mine eye" (Psa. 32:8). With his Word in our hands and his Spirit in our hearts and the light of the knowledge of his glory shining upon us in the face of Jesus Christ, surely we ought not to need the bit and bridle of violent providences to restrain us from willful and headstrong prayers, much less the scourge of terrible chastisement to drive us to pray at all.

So let us enter into the fullness of our blessing in Christ. Knowing that praying in the name of Christ is "praying in the Holy Spirit" (Jude 1:20), the sole and blessed medium of a common life between the saint and his Savior, and that praying in the Holy Spirit is having the Spirit to "help our infirmities," since "we know not what to pray for as we ought;" and to make intercession for us "according to the will of God" (Rom. 8:20-21), how intently shall we seek to learn the highest use of that Divine name by entering into the deepest communion with that Divine Person. And with what earnestness and strength of desire may we constantly plead that prayer of Alexandre Vinet (1797-1847): *"O God, unite more and more closely, not our spirit to a name but our soul to a soul; to the soul of Jesus Christ thy Son and the Son of man, our God, our Brother. In this intimate and living union may this soul gradually become our soul, and may we learn of him by virtue of living with him, to love as he loved, to bless as he blessed, and to pray as he prayed."* Amen.

Source for Chapter 18: A. J. Gordon, *In Christ* (Grand Rapids: Baker, 1964), 134-150. Reprinted from the 1872 edition by Gould and Lincoln, Boston. Retrieved from: http://www.gordon.edu/page.cfm? iPageID=1805.

CHAPTER 19

The Administration of the Spirit

The Holy Ghost from the day of Pentecost has occupied an entirely new position. The whole administration of the affairs of the church of Christ has since that day devolved upon Him. . . . That day was the installation of the Holy Spirit as the Administrator of the church in all things, which office he is to exercise according to circumstances at his discretion. It is as vested with such authority that he gives his name to this dispensation. . . . There is but one other great event to which the Scripture directs us to look, and that is the second coming of the Lord. Till then we live in the Pentecostal age and under the rule of the Holy Ghost.

—James Elder Cumming (1830-1917)

The Holy Spirit, as coming down to fill the place of the ascended Redeemer, has rightly been called "The Vicar of Jesus Christ." To him the entire administration of the church has been committed until the Lord shall return in glory. His oversight extends to the slightest detail in the ordering of God's house, holding all in subjection to the will of the Head, and directing all in harmony with the Divine plan. How clearly this comes out in First Corinthians 12. As in striking a series of concentric circles there is always one fixed center holding each circumference in defined relation to itself, so here we see all the "diversities of administrations" determined by the one Administrator, the Holy Spirit. "Varieties of gifts, but *the same Spirit*"; "diversities of working, but *the same God*"; different words "according to *the same Spirit'*"; "gifts of faith *in the same Spirit*"; "gifts of healing *in the one Spirit*"; miracles, prophecies, tongues, interpretations, "but all these worketh the *one and the same Spirit,* dividing to each one severally as he will." Whether the authority of this one ruling sovereign Holy Spirit be recognized or ignored determines whether the church shall be an anarchy or a unity, a synagogue of lawless ones or the temple of the living God.

Would one desire to find the clue to the great apostasy whose dark eclipse now covers two-thirds of nominal Christendom, here it is—the rule and authority of the Holy Spirit ignored in the church; the servants of the house assuming mastery and encroaching more and more on the prerogatives of the Head, till at last one man sets himself up as the administrator of the church, and daringly usurps the name of "The Vicar of Christ." When the Spirit of the Lord, speaking by Paul, would picture the mystery of lawlessness and the culmination of apostasy, he gives us a description which none should misunderstand: "So that he, as God, sitteth in the temple of God, shewing himself that he is God" (2 Thess. 2:4). What is the temple of God? The church without a question: "Know ye not that ye are the temple of God, and that the Spirit of God dwelleth in you?" (1 Cor. 3:16). Whose prerogative is it to sit there? The Holy Spirit's, its ruler and administrator, and his alone.

When Christ, our Paraclete with the Father, entered upon his ministry on high, we are told more than a score of times that he "sat down at the right hand of God" (e.g., Heb. 12:2). Henceforth heaven is his official seat, until he returns in power and great glory. When he sent down another Paraclete to abide with us for the age, he took his seat in the church, the temple of God, there to rule and to administer till the Lord returns. There is but one "Holy See" upon earth: that is the seat of the Holy One in the church, which only the Spirit of God can occupy without the most daring blasphemy. It becomes all true believers to look well to that picture of one "sitting in the temple of God," and to read the lesson which it teaches. We may have no temptation toward the papacy, which thrusts a man into the seat of the Holy Spirit,[1] or toward clericalism which imposes an order of ecclesiastics—archbishops, cardinals, and archdeacons into that sacred place. But let us remember that a democracy may be guilty of the same sin as a hierarchy, in settling solemn issues by a "show of hands," instead of prayerfully waiting for the guidance of the Holy Spirit, in substituting the voice of a majority for the voice of the Spirit.

Of course, in speaking thusly we concede that the Holy Spirit makes known his will in the voice of believers, as also in the voice of Scripture. Only there must be such prayerful sanctifying of the one and such prayerful search of the other, that in reaching decisions in the church there may be the same declaration as in the first Christian council: "It seemed good to the Holy Spirit and to us" (Acts 15:28).

In some very profound teaching in 2 Corinthians 3, we seem to have a hint as to how we hear the voice of the Lord in guiding the affairs of the church. There the administration (*diakonia*) of the Spirit is distinctly spoken of in contrast with the administration of the law. Its deliverances are written "not with ink, not in tables of stone, but in the tables that are the hearts of flesh, with the Spirit of the living God" (3:3 RV). There must be a sensitive heart wherein this handwriting may be inscribed; an unhindering will through which he may act. "Where the Spirit of the Lord is, there is liberty" (3:17), it is written in the same passage; liberty for God to speak and act as he will through us, which begets loyalty; not liberty for us to act as we will, which begets lawlessness.

To us there is something exceedingly suggestive in the teaching of the Lord's post-ascension gospel, the Revelation, on this point. The epistles to the seven churches we hold, with many of the best commentators, to be a prophetic setting forth of the successive stages of the church's history—its declines and its recoveries, its failures and its repentances, from ascension to advent. And because the Bride of Christ is perpetually betrayed into listening to false teachers and surrendering to the guidance of evil counselors, the Lord is constantly admonishing her to heed the voice of her true Teacher and Guide, the Holy Spirit. How forcibly this admonition is introduced into the great apocalyptic drama! As in the opening of the successive seals, representing the judgments of God upon apostate Christendom, the cry is repeated, "Come"! "Come"! "Come"! "Come"! (Rev. 6)—as though the church under chastisement would repeatedly relearn the advent prayer which her Lord put into her mouth in the beginning: "Even so, come, Lord Jesus" (Rev. 2:20), so at each stage of the church's backsliding a voice is heard from heaven saying: "He that hath an ear, let him hear what the Spirit saith unto the churches" (Rev. 2:7, 11, 17, 29; 3:6, 13, 22). It is the admonition "of him that hath the seven spirits of

God" (Rev. 3:1), seven times addressed to his church throughout her earthly history, calling her to return from her false guides and misleading teachers, and to listen to the voice of her true Counselor.

From this general statement of the administration of the Holy Spirit, let us now proceed to a particular act and office in which this authority is exercised.

The Holy Spirit in the ministry and government of the church. In speaking to the elders of Ephesus, Paul says: "Take heed unto yourselves, and to all the flock in the which the Holy Spirit hath made you bishops, to feed the church of God" (Acts 20:28 RV). Clearly in the beginning, bishops or pastors were given by the Spirit of God, not by the vote of the people. The office and its incumbent were alike by direct Divine appointment. We find this distinctly set forth in the Epistle to the Ephesians: "When he ascended on high, he led captivity captive, and gave gifts unto men. . . . And he gave some to be apostles; and some, prophets; and some, evangelists; and some, pastors and teachers; for the perfecting of the saints, unto the work of ministering, unto the building up of the body of Christ" (Eph. 4:8-12 RV).

The ascent of the Lord and the descent of the Spirit are here exhibited in their necessary relation. In the one event Christ took his seat in heaven as "Head over all things to his church" (Eph. 1:22); in the other the Holy Spirit came down to begin the work of "building up the body of Christ." Of course it is the Head who directs the construction of the body, as being" fitly framed together it groweth into a holy temple in the Lord"; and it is the Holy Spirit who superintends this construction since "we are builded together for an habitation of God in the Spirit" (Eph. 2:21-22).

Therefore all the offices through which this work is to be carried on were appointed by Christ and instituted through the Spirit whom he sent down. Suppose now that men invent offices which are not named in the inspired list, and set up in the church an order of popes and cardinals, archbishops and archdeacons? Is it not a presumption, the worst fruit of which is not alone that it introduces confusion into the body of Christ, but that it begets insubordination to the rule of the Holy Spirit? But suppose, on the other hand, that we sacredly maintain those offices of the ministry which have been established for permanent continuance in the church, and yet take it upon us to fill these according to our own preference and will; is this any less an affront to the Spirit?

Doubtless the mistakes of God's servants, as given in Scripture are as truly designed for our instruction and admonition as their obedient examples. We think we do not err in finding such a recorded warning in the opening chapter of the Acts of the Apostles. A vacancy had occurred in the apostolate. Standing up in the upper room, amidst the hundred and twenty, Peter boldly affirmed that this vacancy must be filled, and of the men who had companied with them during the Lord's earthly ministry, "one must be ordained to be a witness with us of his resurrection" (Acts 1:22).

But the disciples had hitherto had no voice in choosing apostles. The Lord had done this of his own sovereign will: "Have I not chosen you twelve" (John 6:70)? Now he had gone away into heaven, and his Administrator had not yet arrived to enter upon his office work. Surely if the Divine order was to be, that having "ascended on high" he was "to give some apostles," it would be better to await the coming of the Paraclete with his gifts. Not only so, but we are persuaded that, with Christ departed and the Holy Spirit not yet come, a valid election of an apostle was impossible. But in spite of this, a nomination was made; prayer was offered in which the Lord was asked to indicate which of the candidates he had chosen; and then a vote having been taken, Matthias was declared elected. Is there any indication that this choice was ever ratified by the Lord? On the contrary, Matthias passes into obscurity from this time, his name never again being mentioned. Some two years subsequent, the Lord calls Saul of Tarsus; he is sealed with his Spirit, and certified by such evident credentials of the Divine appointment that he boldly signs himself "Paul, an apostle, not of men, neither by man, but by Jesus Christ and God the Father" (Gal. 1:1).

We believe that the apostolic office has passed away, the qualification therefor, that of having been a witness of the Lord's resurrection, being now impossible. But the office of pastor, elder, bishop, or teacher of the flock still remains. And the Divine plan is that this office should be filled, just as in the beginning, by the appointment of the Holy Spirit. Nor can we doubt that if there is a prayerful waiting upon him for guidance, and a sanctified submission to his will when it is made known, he will now choose pastors and set them over their appointed flocks just as manifestly as he did in the beginning.

Very beautiful is the picture in Revelation of the glorified Lord, moving among the candlesticks. There are "seven golden candlesticks" now, not one only as in the Jewish temple. The church of God is manifold, not a unit.[2] He who "walketh in the midst of the seven golden candlesticks" (Rev. 2:1) "holdeth the seven stars in his right hand" (Rev. 1:16). These stars are "the angels of the seven churches" (Rev. 1:20) — their ministers or bishops as generally understood. The Lord holds them in his right hand. Does he not require us to ask of him alone for their bestowal? Yes. "Pray ye therefore the Lord of the harvest, that he would send forth laborers into his harvest" (Luke 10:2).

There is no intimation in Scripture that we are to apply anywhere but to him for the ministry of his church. Does he not give such ministry, and he alone? Yes. "When he ascended on high . . . he gave some . . . pastors and teachers" (Eph. 4:8, 11). And now, speaking to the church in Ephesus, the elders of which, chosen by the Holy Spirit, Paul had so affectionately exhorted, he is seen in the attitude of Chief-shepherd and Bishop-giving pastors with his own hand, placing them with his own right hand, and warning the church that though they have tried and rejected false apostles, they have nevertheless left their "first love" (Rev. 2:4). Significant word! On this love our Lord conditioned the indwelling of the Father and of the Son through the Holy Spirit (John 14:23). Losing this, the peril becomes imminent that the candlestick may be removed out of its place; and so the warning is solemnly announced: "He that hath an ear, let him hear what the Spirit saith unto the churches." Without the Spirit the candlestick can shed forth no light, and loses its place of testimony.

Dead churches, whose witness has been silenced, whose place has been vacated, even though the lifeless form remains, have we not seen such? And what is the safeguard against them, if not that found in the apostle's warning: "Quench not the Spirit" (1 Thess. 5:19)? The voice of the Lord must be heard in his church, and to the Holy Spirit alone has been committed the prerogative of communicating that voice. Is there any likelihood that that voice will be heard when the king or prime minister of a civil government holds the sole function of appointing the bishops, as in the case of state churches? Is there any certainty of it when an archbishop or bishop puts pastors over flocks by the action of his single will? We may congratulate ourselves that we are neither in a state church nor under an episcopal bishop; but there are methods of ignoring or repressing the voice of the Holy Spirit, which though simpler and far less apparent than those just indicated, are no less violent. The humble and godly membership of the little church may turn to some pastor, after much prayer and waiting on God for the Spirit's guidance, and the signs of the Divine choice may be dearly manifest—when some pulpit committee, or some conclave of "leading brethren," vetoes their action on the basis, perchance, that the candidate is not popular and will not draw a crowd. Alas! for the little flock so lorded-over that the voice of the Holy Spirit cannot be heard.

⋅ And majorities are no more to be depended upon than minorities, if there is in both cases a neglect of patient and prolonged waiting upon the Lord to know his will. Of what value is a "show of hands" unless his are stretched out "who holdeth the seven stars in his right hand?" Of what use is a *viva voce* choice, except the living voice of Christ be heard speaking by his Spirit?

One may object that we are holding up an ideal which is impossible to be realized. It is a difficult ideal we admit, as the highest attainments are always difficult; but it is not an impossible one. It is easier to recite our prayers from a book than to read them from the tables of a prepared heart, where the finger of the Spirit has silently written them; but the more difficult way is the more acceptable way to him who seeks for worshipers who "worship in Spirit and in truth" (John 4:24). It is easier to get "the sense of the meeting" in choosing a pastor than to learn "the mind of the Spirit" by patient tarrying and humble surrender to God; but the more laborious way will certainly prove the more profitable way. The failure to take this way is, we are persuaded, the cause of more decay and spiritual death in the churches than we have yet imagined.

From the watchtower where we write we can look out on half a score of churches on which "Ichabod" (1 Sam. 4:21) has been evidently written, and the glory of which has long since departed. They were founded in prayer and consecration, "to serve the living and true

God, and to wait for his Son from heaven" (1 Thess. 1:9-10). Why has their light been extinguished, though the lampstand which once bore it still remains, adorned and beautified with all that the highest art and architecture can suggest? Their history is known to him who walks among the golden candlesticks. What violence may have been done, by headstrong self-will, to him who is called "the Spirit of counsel and might" (Isa. 11:2). What rejection of the truth which he, "the Spirit of truth" (John 14:17; 15:26; 16:13) has appointed for the faith of God's church till at last the word has been spoken: "Ye do always resist the Holy Spirit; as your fathers did, so do ye" (Acts 7:51).

Is it only Jewish worshipers to whom these words apply? Is it only a Jewish temple of which this sentence is true: "Behold your house is left unto you desolate" (Matt. 23:38)? The Spirit will not be entirely withdrawn from the body of Christ indeed, but there is the *Church*, and there are *churches*. A man may yet live and breathe when cell after cell has been closed by congestion till at last he only inhales and exhales with a little portion of one lung. Let him that reads understand.

The Spirit is the breath of God in the body of his church. While that Divine body survives and must, multitudes of churches have so shut out the Spirit from rule and authority and supremacy in the midst of them that the ascended Lord can only say to them: "Thou hast a name that thou livest, and art dead" (Rev. 3:1). In a word, so vital and indispensable is the ministry of the Spirit, that without it nothing else will avail. Some trust in creeds, and some in ordinances; some suppose that the church's security lies in a sound theology, and others locate it in a primitive simplicity of government and worship; but it lies in none of these, desirable as they are. The body may be as to its organs perfect and entire, lacking nothing; but simply because the Spirit has been withdrawn from it, it has passed from a church into a corpse. As one has powerfully stated it:

> When the Holy Spirit withdraws . . . he sometimes allows the forms which he has created to remain. The oil is exhausted, but the lamp is still there; prayer is offered and the Bible read; church-going is not given up, and to a certain degree the ser-

vice is enjoyed; in a word, religious habits are preserved, and like the corpses found at Pompeii, which were in a perfect state of preservation and in the very position in which death had surprised them, but which were reduced to ashes by contact with the air, so the blast of trial, of temptation, or of final judgment will destroy these spiritual corpses.[3]

Source for Chapter 19: A. J. Gordon, *The Ministry of the Spirit* (Philadelphia: American Baptist Publication Society, 1896), 128-142.

CHAPTER 20

Healing: Remarkable Answers to Prayer

"One thing I know, that whereas I was blind I now see" (John 9:25). This confession of experience has always been regarded as the strongest that can be made. The "I know" indeed may seem to savor of egotism and assurance. But let us not forget that while the egotism of opinion is always offensive, the egotism of experience can never be rebuked. It is the highest attainment of mere human thought and speculation to know that one does not know.
                                                    — A. J. Gordon, *The Ministry of Healing*

I have little to say in regard to the principles of Divine healing," A. J. Gordon says in a letter, "but am looking constantly for light. It is a subject full of difficulties, and I shrink more and more from undertaking any philosophy of it. I do my best with every case which comes before me."[1]

When the sick sought him out he prayed with them in quietness and reserve. Many remarkable answers have been preserved.

Editor: These testimonies are recorded in a biography written by his son, Ernest B. Gordon. See source material at chapter's end.

Testimonial:
Rev. Joseph C. Young, Boston, Massachusetts

In 1887 there appeared a growth on my lip. When first noticed it was very small, but gradually increased until it seriously interfered with my preaching. A physician of good standing, after two examinations, told me that it was cancer and that I had better put my house in order, as he believed I had only a short time to live.

Though believing in healing by faith, I had no appropriating faith to claim the promise *for myself,* yet I constantly sought Divine guidance. For a week I had no light. At the end of this time the promise in James 5:14 came into my mind like a new revelation. I had read and quoted it to others hundreds of times, but now it came direct to me with an indescribable force. I believed it immediately. Then came a perplexity—who were the elders of the church? Who could offer the prayer of faith for me? I knew many in Brooklyn, my home, and in New York, who professed faith in this promise, but I had no inclination to call them.

I made the matter a subject of special prayer for some days, and the name of Dr. Gordon, with whom I was only slightly acquainted, was so vividly thrust into my mind that I accepted it as an answer to my prayer. The appointment was made to meet him in Boston with Mr. McElwain and Dr. Peck. I told them why I had come, and asked if they could take the promise in James and pray in faith for my healing. They replied that they could, and Dr. Gordon prayed, anointing me according to the instructions. I was in the study only a short time, and went away almost immediately after the prayer. I had no more pain or trouble from the cancer, and within a few weeks all signs of it had disappeared. It has never returned. The promise was believed, the prayer was offered, I was healed. . . . I give this testimony with some reluctance. It is not a subject to be too much advertised. The Spirit heals according to the will of God, not according to our will. There has been too much fleshly formulating of theories on this as on all other teachings of the Bible, and for that reason less of the power of God manifested.

Testimonial:
Mr. Mial Davis, a lumber-merchant of Fitchburg, Massachusetts

Next to my conversion, the Divine healing in the study of dear Dr. Gordon was the most remarkable experience of my life. In 1889 I was prostrated. The right thigh seemed to lose its vitality to such a degree that it seemed for a time impossible to bring life back to it. Some of my friends wished to remove me to the Massachusetts General Hospital to see if amputation could not save me. I said no; I was ready to die. Years of prostration followed. At intervals I could go about with crutch or cane; at other times I was confined to my bed. I could do little or nothing at my business. My mind finally turned to the study of healing by faith. After correspondence I forced myself, in great weakness, on crutches to Dr. Gordon's study. He laid his hand upon my heart and, oh, what a prayer for my recovery, what pleading with God! Brother McElwain's prayer followed, then my own poor prayer. Oh, what a miniature transfiguration of Jesus was there! The very place was holy ground. That was the day of days to me. You probably know how I went "walking and leaping, praising God." I rose from my knees after all of us had prayed, went out on the sidewalk to go to the depot. I felt that new life had come to my knee and limb from thigh to foot. I walked up and down the [rail] cars while on my way home, praising God and giving him the glory. I had worn rubber bands round my knee, leg, and ankle, but the next morning I did not put them on and never have worn them since. My crutches and cane were laid aside. I have been able to do far more church work and business than ever I expected to do.

Testimonial:
Miss Emma Davis, Southboro, Massachusetts

I suffered for years from seasons of utter prostration and acute suffering, with insomnia frequent and prolonged. My left side was a little, weak, shrunken thing, and my spine was badly curved, the right side being much too large and bowed. A few years since, when my attention was called to the Lord's healing, I was about as full of unbelief and prejudice as one could be. But prejudice began to melt away under the light of the Word, and I began to believe that possibly I might be helped. I consecrated myself to God as never before. Dear friends prayed earnestly in my behalf, and as fully as I knew how, I placed my case in the hands of the great Physician. For a while I was better. Then new ills came upon me until it seemed at times as though my very reason would leave me. . . . About this time I was most definitely led to write to Dr. Gordon. An interview followed. He seemed fearful lest I should fix my faith on the human agency instead of on the Divine. He said most emphatically, "I have no power." But, replied I, "You have faith in the One who has." He smiled, and asked some very searching questions as to my faith to receive, as to consecration, and the use of God-given health.

He appointed a day when he would with others pray with me for my healing. When I came to his study I was suffering intensely. With others he prayed for me, placing his hands on my head. I felt no change. Reaching home, I was soon prostrated with the old misery, suffering terribly night and day for nearly two weeks, but over and over again came to me the words, "Fear not, only believe"; and there was a deep stillness and peace in my soul, beyond anything I had ever experienced. The trial of faith was fiery, but I knew deliverance was near.

One morning about the middle of April, I woke without a pain in my body, and as I then expressed it, "they are all carried away into the wilderness." With a new song in my heart, even praises to God, and with faithful promises, I rose up to serve anywhere the Lord might indicate. It is now almost four years, and I have had no return of my old pains or sickness. The change in my deformity is most marked. All the pads and artificial means of relief are dispensed with. . . . Until my healing I was always over-tired, and the more tired the more pain and insomnia. Now no matter how much I exert myself I wake fresh and rested in the mornings. . . . Can anyone explain away this sudden lifting of nearly thirty years' misery?

Testimonial:
Mrs. Gertrude Floyd Cole (deceased), statement of husband

She was a fragile girl from her youth up, a few days at school being sufficient to exhaust her for weeks. Yet she was ever a person of great piety and of a pronounced spiritual life. Coming to Boston, she found work as a sewing-woman. The confinement brought on consumption of the most malignant type, accompanied by severe hemorrhages. The physician pronounced her case hopeless. Dr. Gordon, on one of his visits, the last preceding his departure to the country, conversed with the dying girl. He asked her if she could rely on the Lord Jesus Christ to raise her up, human aid having done all in its power. She said that she could, and that henceforth she surrendered herself to Christ. He prayed the prayer of faith as recorded in James, and left her in God's hands. She . . . sank beyond all indications of life, and was pronounced to have passed away. She did indeed pass into the world of eternal life, and heard, that which cannot be recorded other than that she was told that her life-work was not yet complete.

While the attendants were making ready for her burial, she showed signs of returning life. From that hour her hemorrhages ceased and a warm and grateful healing sensation permeated her lungs, and she was raised to health. Dr. Gordon, on returning from the country in the fall, met her on the street and did not know her, so perfectly had she recovered. This was his first intimation of her healing. She lived many years, married, engaged in Christian work, and died finally, though not of consumption.

Source for Chapter 20: Ernest B. Gordon, *Adoniram Judson Gordon: A Biography* (New York: Fleming H. Revell Company, 1896), 143-148. Retrieved from: http://www.gordon.edu/page.cfm?iPageID=1805.

CHAPTER 21

Behold, He Cometh!

The second coming of Christ is the axis of a true eschatology, that in which all its doctrines and all its hopes stand together.

— A. J. Gordon

I t is such a momentous event—the coming of the Son of Man in the clouds of heaven—and the contemplation of it so overpowers the imagination, that we can easily understand why, in this age so averse to the supernatural, attempts to explain away its literalness should multiply on every hand.

But, as though anticipating these evasions and advancements of latter-day philosophy, the Holy Spirit has guarded this great hope of the church. By the utmost accuracy of definition: "this same Jesus who is taken up from you"—fixes the corporeal identity of the coming Lord with him whom we have known of the wounded hands and pierced feet; and "shall so come in like manner as ye have seen him go into Heaven" (Acts 1:11)—determines his literal, visible, and bodily return to earth. So, it is also, with the Thessalonian prediction. In the words, "the Lord himself shall descend from heaven with a shout" (1 Thess. 4:16), there is a kind of underscoring of Holy Writ, that we may be particularly reminded that it is no spiritual apparition of Christ for which we look, but "his own august personal presence."

And yet his *parousia*, of which the Scripture so constantly speaks, is said to signify his presence; and therefore elaborate volumes have been written to prove that "the coming (*parousia*) of the Son of Man" means his abiding invisible dwelling in the church through the Holy

Spirit. "Presence" the word undoubtedly means, but not *omnipresence.* The *everywhereness* of Christ in the person of the Comforter is the peculiar blessing of this dispensation. In this sense he can say to every member of his mystical body, the church, in every place on earth and at every moment of time: "lo, I am with you always, even unto the end of the age" (Matt. 28:20). It was in order to give place for this worldwide, or rather church-wide, indwelling that it was expedient for our Lord to go away, that so the Paraclete might come to abide with his people perpetually. But this everywhere-presence of Christ by the Holy Spirit is never once spoken of in Scripture as his *parousia.* This term applies only to his bodily and visible presence, a being with us, which can only be effected by a corporeal return to us. Therefore is his advent comprehensively called his *parousia,* or coming; it is that for which we look, and which "every eye shall see" (Rev. 1:7), and not that which has already come to pass spiritually, and which, therefore, no eye can see.

The second coming of Christ is the axis of a true eschatology, that in which all its doctrines and all its hopes stand together. Rightly are some insisting on what they name a Christo-centric theology; only let them consistently apply their principle to the doctrine of last things, making all our ultimate hopes and attainments to concenter in the coming Christ. Then shall we cease to hear in orthodox dogmatics that "sanctification ends at death," when the New Testament everywhere binds its consummation to the second advent of Christ. Then, also, except in liberal theology, may we no longer listen to the affirmation that resurrection is attained for each one separately in an instant, in the shutting of an eye, at the last breath of the body, when Scripture declares that "we shall all be changed, in a moment, in the twinkling of an eye, at the last trump" (1 Cor. 15:51-52).

Any doctrine of the resurrection dissociated from the advent must be false—false because eccentric, and without relation to the axis of redemption, the *parousia.* No atonement apart from the cross; no resurrection apart from the coming! The morning star of the church is the glorious appearing; but this star, at least, has satellites—the resurrection, the rapture, the glory—and not one of these will be visible "until the day dawn, and the day star arise" (2 Pet. 1:19).

What deep questions suggest themselves as soon as we begin to meditate on this theme! How can it be, if his coming is personal and bodily, that "*every* eye shall see him"? Will his *parousia* be prolonged, or, as some hold, will it elapse in a moment, "as the lightning cometh out of the east, and shineth even unto the west" (Matt. 24:27), leaving the great world to wonder what has become of the saints? In other words, will he be visible to his church alone at his *parousia*, manifesting himself unto them, but not to the world until a later epiphany, when he shall appear in glory with his saints? Already there has been too much of dogmatizing on these points; therefore we prefer to leave them for the day to reveal.

The attitude of the church toward this sublime event is the all-important consideration. That should be one of joyful hope, and not of dread expectation. We cannot think that true and watchful believers will share in that advent wail which is so graphically pictured in the Revelation: "All the tribes of the land shall mourn over him" (Rev. 1:7); indeed, they who pierced him, reading their condemnation in his wounds and smiting on their breasts; but they who own those wounds as the credentials of their peace with God will lift up their heads and rejoice, saying: "Lo, this is our God; we have waited for him and he will save us: this is the Lord; we have waited for him; we will be glad and rejoice in his salvation" (Isa. 25:9). Eagerly do we summon parable and poetry to picture the exultant scene as we gather it from Scripture. Dr. Andrew Bonar, who stands among us, as the venerable Simeon of our generation, "just and devout, waiting for the consolation of Israel" (Luke 2:25), has, in a recent message, made the advent scene so real by the use of a historical incident, that we are constrained to reproduce the picture entirely:

> When those that upheld the banner of truth had almost lost heart, and Protestantism seemed failing, John Knox accepted the invitation from the true-hearted ones, and left Geneva for Scotland. When he landed, quick as lightning the news spread abroad. The cry arose everywhere, "John Knox has come!" Edinburgh came rushing into the streets; the old and the young, the lordly and the low, were seen mingling together in delighted expectation. All business, all common

pursuits, were forsaken. The priests and friars abandoned their altars and their masses and looked out alarmed, or were seen standing by themselves, shunned like lepers. Studious men were roused from their books; mothers set down their infants and ran to inquire what had come to pass. Travelers suddenly mounted and sped into the country with the tidings, "John Knox has come." At every cottage door the inmates stood and clustered, wondering, as horseman after horseman cried, "Knox has come." Boats departing from the harbor bore up to each other at sea to tell the news. Shepherds heard the tidings as they watched their flocks upon the hills. The warders in the castle challenged the sound of quick feet approaching, and the challenge was answered, "John Knox has come!" The whole land was moved; the whole country was stirred with a new inspiration, and the hearts of enemies withered.

Oh, if that was the effect of the sudden presence of a man like ourselves—a man whom we will rejoice to meet in the kingdom, but only a man—what will the land feel, what will earth feel, when the news comes, *"The Son of man! The Son of man!"* His sign has been seen in the heaven! O wise virgins, with what joy will you go out to meet him!

Some admonish us not to take too literally the words, "And at midnight there was a cry made, Behold the Bridegroom cometh!" (Matt. 25:6) since, sudden as the advent surprise will be, it cannot really be in the night for all the world, as one side of the globe is dark and the other light at the same moment. True, and yet how perfectly our Lord's picture of his coming answers to this fact, since it brings into the same instantaneous photograph a day-scene, and a night-scene, and a twilight-scene: "I tell you in that night there shall be two men in one bed"—the midnight surprise; "the one shall be taken and the other shall be left." "Two women shall be grinding together"—the twilight surprise; "the one shall be taken and the other left." "Then shall two be in the field"—the midday surprise; "the one shall be taken and the other left" (Matt. 24:40; Luke 17:34-36). It would seem thus as though the lightning flash of his *parousia* would encircle the world in an instant. Realistic in the highest degree is the picture: no halt in the hurried march of our humanity for burnishing the armor for the grand review; no pause in life's drama for shifting the scenery before the final act is introduced! Instant transition of the church from busy toil and tired sleep into the beatific vision and the awakening immortality, and as instant a lapse of the ungodly from the day of grace into the day of doom. The event will evidently be utterly unexpected except for the faithful few who have kept their watch.

Morally, or rather dispensationally, Christ's coming will be in the night. For such, according to Scripture, is the whole period of our Lord's absence. When he was yet with his church he said: "I must work the works of him that sent me while it is day: "the night cometh" (John 9:4). It was his presence that made the day — "As long as I am in the world, I am the light of the world" (John 9:5) — and his departure that would bring the night. Hence we find Paul saying — in the time of the Lord's absence and in view of his return — "The night is far spent, the day is at hand" (Rom. 13:12). Here is an exact inversion of the order from that of Christ, suggesting that it is the absence or the presence of our Lord which determines the question. "They that sleep, sleep in the night" (1 Thess. 5:6). The words are true dispensationally as well as literally. So long as "they that sleep in Jesus" (1 Thess. 4:14) are still in their graves, the world's morning will not have come: "And they that are drunken are drunken in the night" (1 Thess. 5:7).

So long as the riot of unrestrained sin goes on over all the earth, and the mass of humanity is held in the mad intoxication of the god of this world, the day-dawn will not yet be visible. But what an exquisite parable there is for us — an enacted parable — in that story of Christ's walking on Tiberias! He has "gone up unto the mountain apart to pray," and the church which he launched is "now in the midst of the sea, tossed with waves and the wind contrary." But "in the fourth watch of the night" he comes to her, walking upon the sea; and they, who for a moment feared and were troubled at the startling apparition, will hear his voice saying, "Be of good cheer: it is I; be not afraid" (Matt. 14:23-27). These words will bring an end to all sorrow, a calm for all storms.

"And they shall see the Son of man coming in the clouds of heaven with power and great glory" (Matt. 24:30). Jesus has said this concerning himself, and to attempt to heighten the effect of his words by any imaginative description of the scene predicted were certainly to lower the impression which the inspired declaration itself makes upon the mind. So great is this saying that it alone befits the incarnate Word who spoke it. "Only a Jesus could forge a Jesus," it has been said; and only the Coming One whom we have known, "whose goings forth have been of old from everlasting" (Micah 5:2) could predict for himself such a coming as this. And the hope of it has reversed the current of humanity.

"Man *goeth* to his long home, and the mourners go about the streets" (Eccl. 12:5), was the plaintive strain of the old dispensation. But since Jesus ascended and put the exultant *Ecce Venit* into the mouth of his redeemed, "Man *cometh*" is now their song. The procession of mortality is about to halt, and then to move forward; but forward shall now signify from death to life: from the pilgrim's inn of the grave to the long home of "forever with the Lord." (1 Thess. 4:17).

Source for Chapter 20: A. J. Gordon, *Ecce Venit: Behold He Cometh* (New York: Fleming H. Revell Company, 1889), 208-217. Retrieved from: http://www.gordon.edu/page.cfm?iPageID=1805.

Endnotes

Editor: These Endnotes, with the exception of my Introduction and an explanation under Chapter 20, are recorded as they appear in A. J. Gordon's respective works, with some editorial corrections.

Introduction
1. A. J. Gordon, *Ecce Venit: Behold He Cometh* (New York: Fleming H. Revell, 1889), 208.
2. Ernest B. Gordon, *Adoniram Judson Gordon: A Biography* (New York: Fleming H. Revell, 1896), 94.
3. Ibid., 95.
4. Ibid., 95.

Chapter 3: How Christ Came to Church: Here Today
1. H. C. G. Moule, *Veni Creator: Thought on the Person and Work of the Holy Spirit of Promise* (London: Hodder and Stroughton, 1895), 13.
2. Joseph Hart, "Come, Holy Spirit, Come!"
3. Augustine, *Epistles*, p. 29.

Chapter 9: The Advent of the Spirit
1. G. F. Tophel, *The Work of the Holy Spirit in Man*, p. 32.
2. William Archer Butler: "Christ having reached his goal, and not till then, bequeaths to his followers the graces that invested his earthly course; the ascending Elijah leaves his mantle behind him. It is only an extension of the same principle, that the declared office of the Holy Spirit being to complete the image of Christ in every faithful follower by effecting in this world a spiritual death and resurrection—a point attested in every epistle—the image could not be stamped until the reality had been wholly accomplished; the Divine Artist could not fitly descend to make the copy before the entire original had been provided."
3. Ambrose: "Because though he and the Father are one, and the Father his Father by the propriety of nature, to us God became a Father through the

Son, not by right of nature, but by grace."

Chapter 10: The Conviction of the Spirit
1. Thomas Cartwright: "For as the ministry of Enoch was sealed by his reception into heaven, and as the ministry of Elijah was also abundantly proved by his translation, so also the righteousness and innocence of Christ. But it was necessary that the ascension of Christ should be more fully attested, because upon his righteousness, so fully proved by his ascension, we must depend for all our righteousness. For if God had not approved him after his resurrection, and he had not taken his seat at his right hand, we could by no means be accepted of God."

Chapter 11: The Spirit of Life: Our Regeneration
1. John Milton probably gives the true genesis of this doctrine in these words, which he puts into the mouth of Satan:
   The son of God I also am or was;
   And if I was, I am; relation stands;
   All men are sons of God.
2. Andrew Jukes, *The New Man*, p. 53.

Chapter 12: Regeneration and Renewal
1. Source not cited.
2. Christmas Evans, *Life and Labors*, p. 28.
3. David Brainerd, *The Memoirs of David Brainerd*, p. 46.
4. June 27, 1832, *Life of David Brainerd*. "Most wonderful man! What conflicts, what depressions, desertions, strength, advancement, victories within thy torn bosom! I cannot express what I think when I think of thee. Tonight more set on missionary enterprise than ever" (*Robert Murray McCheyne, Journal*).

Chapter 13: The Embodying of the Spirit
1. Allan Beecher Webb, *The Presence and Office of the Spirit*. "The Holy Spirit not only dwells in the church as his habitation, hut also uses her as the living organism whereby he moves and walks forth in the world, and speaks to the world and acts upon the world. He is the soul of the church which is Christ's body," p. 17.

Chapter 14: Conversion and Consecration
1. William Reid, *The Blood of Jesus,* "The gospel of the grace of God does not consist in pressing the duty defined by the words *'Give your heart to Christ,'* although that is often unwisely urged upon inquirers after salvation as though it were the gospel. The true gospel is, *'Accept the free gift of salvation from wrath and sin by receiving Jesus Himself and all the benefits He purchased with His* blood,'" p. 22.
2. Stevens, *History of Methodism*, vol. 1, p. 105.

3. William Guest, *Life of Stephen Grellet*, p. 3.
4. John Bunyan.
5. *Memorials of Frances R. Havergal*, p. 10.
6. John Howe. In his discourse on self-dedication, he tells of a devout French nobleman who made a quit claim deed of himself to God, and signed the document with his own blood, "whose affection I commend," he adds, "more than his expression of it." And well he might. When God takes security He wants a good name and a trustworthy signature. We are only safe when we present "the name above every name," and trust alone in "the blood of the New Testament."
7. *Life of Oberlin*, p. 26.

Chapter 15: The Enduement of the Spirit

1. Rev. E. Boys, *Filled with the Spirit*, p. 87.
2. Andre Jukes, *The New Man*. "It is assumed by some that because those that walked with Christ of old received the baptism of the Holy Ghost and fire at Pentecost, more than eighteen hundred years ago, therefore all believers now have received the same. As well might the apostles, when first called, have concluded that because at his baptism the Spirit like a dove rested upon Christ, therefore they had equally received the same blessing. Surely the Spirit has been given and the work in Christ wrought for all; but to enter into possession, to be enlightened and made partakers of the Holy Ghost, there must be a personal application to the Lord, etc."
3. William Kelly, *Lectures on the New Testament Doctrine of the Holy Spirit*, p. 161.
4. James Elder Cumming, *Through the Eternal Spirit*. "It is a great mistake into which some have fallen, to suppose that the results of Pentecost were chiefly miraculous and temporary. The effect of such a view is to keep spiritual influences out of sight; and it will be well ever to hold fast the assurance that a wide, deep, and perpetual spiritual blessing in the church is that which above all things else was secured by the descent of the Spirit after Christ was glorified."

Chapter 16: Sanctification in Christ

1. Francis de Sales, *Spiritual Letters*. He writes to one who complains of sad heart sickness over the evil of an unsanctified will: "Thank God, 'this sickness is not unto death, but for the glory *of* God.' You are like Rebecca when two peoples struggled within her womb, *but the younger was destined to prevail. Self-love only dies with our natural death;* it has a thousand wiles whereby to keep a hold within the soul, and we cannot drive it forth. It is the first-born of the soul; it is upheld by a legion of auxiliaries, emotions, actions, inclinations, passions; it is adroit, and knows how to employ endless subtleties. On the other hand, the love of God, which is later born, has its emotions, actions, inclinations, and passions. These two struggle within us, and their convulsive movements cause us infinite trouble. But the love

of God must triumph" (Ch. 12).
2. Adelaide Newton.

Chapter 18: Prayer in Christ
1. Hermann Olshausen: "Name used in application to God and to Christ as the manifestation of God—always denotes the entity itself in the whole compass of its properties. Accordingly prayer in the name of Christ, is such as is offered in the nature, mind, and spirit of Christ." Rudolf Stier: "We pray in the *name*, that is, actually in the person of Christ, that is, as standing in his place through his preparatory and intercessory supplication, as if He came in and with us and Himself prayed what we ask. Nor is this a mere *as if*, rather it is the essential truth of the matter."
2. Johann Neander, "Having previously said that prayer in the name of Christ is ever heard by the Father, he now adds the condition that we pray according to his will. The one is involved in the other, as we have already shown. He who prays in the name of Christ is moved and guided by the Spirit of Christ in prayer. He can ask for nothing but that which is in accordance with the will of God; can with assurance ask only that which the Spirit of Christ makes known to him in prayer as corresponding to the Father's will. When this certainty is lacking, his prayer will always be accompanied with the condition that the desire arising in his soul and taking the form of prayer, may have for its object something which the Father approves" (1 John 5:14).
3. See the thoughtful essay on *Prayer Considered in its Relation to the Will of Man and in its Dependence on the Sacrifice of Christ's Death,* by Dora Greenwell, to whom I am indebted for I know not how many suggestions of truth.
4. Bishop Wilson, *Sacra Privata.*
5. Friedrich Krummacher.
6. John McLeod Campbell, *Christ the Bread of Life.* Prayer in Christ is "the Eternal Life which comes to us through the Son, ascending from us through the Son, the Son in us honoring the Father, the worship of Sonship as such grateful to the Father, who seeketh such worship. Freedom and confidence of acknowledgment are of the very nature of such worship; arising necessarily from the oneness of the Spirit, causing oneness of mind and will in the worshippers and in Him who is worshipped. In such worship there is a continual living presentation of Christ to the Father, a continual drawing upon the delights of the Father in the Son, the outgoing of a confidence that, whatever is asked in Christ's name, in the light of his name, in the faith of the Father's acknowledgment of that name, will be received. The praises rendered, the desires cherished, the prayers offered, are all within the circle of the life of Christ, and ascend with the assurance of partaking in the favor which pertains to that life, which rests upon Him who is that life," p. 130.

Chapter 19: The Administration of the Spirit

1. Of course Catholic writers claim that the pope is the "Vicar of Christ" only as being the mouthpiece of the Holy Ghost. But the Spirit has been given to the church as a whole, that is to the body of regenerated believers, and to every member of that body according to his measure. The sin of sacerdotalism is, that it arrogates for a usurping few that which belongs to every member of Christ's mystical body. It is a suggestive fact that the name *klaeros*, which Peter gives to the church as the "flock of God," when warning the elders against being *lords over God's heritage*, now appears in ecclesiastical usage as the *clergy*, with its orders of pontiff and prelates and lord bishops, whose appointed function it is to exercise lordship over Christ's flock.

2. Canon Garratt, *Commentary on the Revelation*. "By the candlesticks being seven instead of one, as in the tabernacle, we are taught that whereas in the Jewish dispensation, God's visible church was one, in the Gentile dispensation there are many visible churches; and that Christ himself recognizes them alike," p. 32.

3. G. F. Tophel, *The Work of the Holy Spirit in Man*, p. 66.

Chapter 20: Healing: Remarkable Answers to Prayer

1. *Editor*: While Gordon says in this letter, "I have little to say in regard to the principles of Divine healing," I'm assuming the book he published on the subject came out at a date later than when he made this statement, for in the book he has a great deal to say about the subject. The book: A. J. Gordon, *The Ministry of Healing*, third edition, revised (New York: Fleming H. Revell, 1882).

CPSIA information can be obtained
at www.ICGtesting.com
Printed in the USA
LVOW13s0043210617
538754LV00018BA/258/P